Fighters
&
Writers

MONGREL EMPIRE PRESS
NORMAN, OKLAHOMA, UNITED STATES OF AMERICA

WWW.MONGRELEMPIREPRESS.COM

This publisher is a proud member of

[clmp]

COUNCIL OF LITERARY MAGAZINES & PRESSES
w w w . c l m p . o r g

Founding Member
OKLAHOMA
SMALL PRESS
ASSOCIATION

Photographs by
Nancy J. Rodwan
(pgs. xi, 37, 42 & 162, cover photo of speed bag, & author photo)

AP/Wide World Photos
(pgs. 59, 72, 94 & 176)
AP/Wide World Photos used by permission.

Cover Design©JLC Mish, 2010

Book Design: Mongrel Empire Press using iWork Pages.

Fighters & Writers

John G. Rodwan, Jr.

MONGREL EMPIRE PRESS NORMAN, OK

In memory of

José Torres

(1936-2009)

TABLE OF CONTENTS

Introduction..3

Part I: Ali & Others
The Ali Act...1

Seeing Stars..17

The Cinderella Man Fairytale 27

Part II: Red & Blue Corners
Health & Safety...35

There are No Easy Answers............................41

A First-Class Sport 45

Part III: Writers & Fighters
Rollins on the Road...57

Going Off Course 61

with Melville & Liebling..................................61

Dedicated Writers 75

The Fighting Life 83

Is Martin Amis Serious? 105

Write, Repeat 117

George & Me 131

Part IV: Fighting Inside
Ink 145

Weight Loss: A Love Story 157

Part V: Fighters & Writers
Fighters & Writers 171

Sources 185

Index..203

INTRODUCTION

One night in 1965, fighter José Torres borrowed writer Norman Mailer's car. After Torres ran a red light, the police stopped him and asked for the registration, which he could not find. At the station, a sergeant called Mailer's mother, who said her son would never have let anyone drive his car, which resulted in Torres being arrested. Later that same year, Mailer took his mother to visit Torres as the boxer prepared for his next bout. On the way there, Mailer warned her to beware of the Puerto Rican, who, he said, might become violent. However, when they met, Torres told the novelist's visibly afraid parent that he respected her for looking out for her son and hoped his mother would have done the same thing for him. Relieved, she hugged him.

Such is the gist of the story as Charlie LeDuff recounts it in *Work and Other Sins*, but when I heard Torres tell it there was more to it. After a night of fights at Madison Square Garden, Mailer and others wanted to go out partying, but Torres was too tired and simply wanted to head home to Brooklyn. If it was March 30, Torres's fatigue would have been entirely understandable. His friends would have been going out to celebrate his having just won the world light heavyweight championship. When the police asked Mailer's mother about her son's Rolls Royce, she pointedly replied that he never would have loaned it to a Puerto Rican. Later, on the way to the training camp in upstate New York, when Mailer cautioned her about the dark-skinned, temperamental fighter, his practical joking played on prejudices she had already voiced. More than a simple misunderstanding that Mailer tried to have some fun with by making his mother anxious before introducing her to the friendly and forgiving fighter, the short but suggestive tale of the boxer's arrest for driving the novelist's car entails issues of race, trust, identity, trickery, loyalty and fear.

That's the special thing about boxing stories: there's always more to them. The car-borrowing anecdote became part of raconteur Torres's repertoire, and he tailored it to suit the occasion and the audience. In LeDuff's version, he added a punch line. Despite their embrace, according to Torres, "Later in life, when she gave an interview, [Mailer's mother] called me a no-good bum. How do you like that?" He concluded with a different ironic reversal when he told me the story. He implied the likelihood of his being pulled over because a man who looked like him automatically attracted suspicion by driving a fancy automobile late at night in the mid-1960s. The protective mother's response to the police's inquiry confirmed racism's role in the incident. Around the time of his greatest professional achievement, Torres suffers the indignity of being treated like a criminal because of his appearance. (Torres told Mailer biographer Peter Manso a slightly different version, in which the car is a customized Mercedes-Benz and the incident occurs later in the year.)

Recognizing that there may be more to boxing stories than just entertaining tales of violence involving distinctive characters, writers find deep reservoirs of meaning, narrative possibility and historical significance in them, whether they involve actual fights or, as with Torres using Mailer's car, they have to do with boxers doing something other than fighting. Whether they, like Mailer, posit a parallel between what they do and what boxers do or they, like Joyce Carol Oates, reject this view, countless writers have pondered the relationship between themselves and fighters. Innumerable authors use boxing as a way into contemplation of other topics, large and small.

Muhammad Ali ranks as the ultimate example of a boxer whose story has more to it than only what he accomplished as an athlete. Long after Ali became a celebrity, writers continue to wrestle with the meaning of pugilism's Proteus, whose astonishing versatility made him a special sort of public figure who embodied multiple, conflicting qualities. He was the undeniably effective boxer who did everything wrong. He was the violent opponent of war. He was beauty and he was ugliness. He was hate and he was love. Not many celebrities can juggle so many identities. "The Ali Act" tries to get a hold on several of the divergent approaches writers have taken in their effort to understand the significance of the exceptionally famous fighter; "Seeing Stars" looks at films about both Ali and another intriguing character, Mike Tyson.

Seeing boxers as having a special capacity to become emblematic figures for their time, writers have also made efforts to mold heroes using far less promising material than Muhammad Ali. During the Great Depression, many observers easily identified with James J. Braddock's impoverishment and his efforts to overcome it. However, his financial problems did not make him a magnificent athlete. His unlikely rise to the heavyweight championship practically begged to be spun as an inspirational story, and some writers could not resist using the clichés it set before them, as I describe in "The Cinderella Man Fairytale." Braddock did not stand long on the pedestal onto which he climbed. In his first attempt to defend his title, he was deposed by a legendary fighter with far stronger claims for greatness, Joe Louis.

Louis not only held onto his championship title for a dozen years and defended it more than two dozen times; he also engaged in a fight that became a hinge event in history. His second bout against Max Schmeling – a fight immediately before the outbreak of World War II against a fighter associated with Nazi Germany – spotlighted him in an episode shining bright with symbolism. As major boxing shows often do, this one involved matters of national and racial identity. "In the eyes of most Americans, Joe Louis had exploded the myth of white supremacy" by beating Schmeling in 1938, according to biographer Chris Mead. "In the process he had won a measure of acceptance as America's national representative, something no black had ever enjoyed before."

Writers routinely overload fighters like Louis, Ali and even Braddock with insupportable symbolic burdens, but some do express reservations about the practice. "Those who write about boxing often work too hard to find high-minded reasons for the visceral pleasure they take in watching two total strangers try to batter one another senseless," Geoffrey C. Ward writes in *Unforgivable Blackness*, his biography of Jack Johnson, another boxer compelled to carry a heavy representational mantle as the first black American heavyweight champion. In railing against this tendency, Ward leans too far the other way, exaggerating the atavistic brutality involved in boxing. Fighters are not always "total strangers." Opponents often know each other. Plenty of boxers end up fighting former sparring partners. Rivals in the ring may even call each other friends outside it. "Boxing is that way," boxer Jimmy Ellis mused in connection with his relationship with Ali. "You know, you can run together, talk together, and wind up fighting each other the next night; but when the fight is over, you shake hands and be friends." Further, as anyone who has seen tactical fights in which the dominant contestant strives to win on points rather than try for a crowd-pleasing knockout can attest, boxers do not invariably aim "to batter one another senseless." Still, Ward does make a valid point, which sportswriter Hugh McIlvanney puts more precisely when he calls boxing "the only activity designated a sport in which participants are officially encouraged to knock their competitors unconscious, to inflict what Spanish speaking fighters call the little death." Another writer, Carlo Rotella, phrases it even more concisely: "Boxers hurt each other on purpose...." Whatever significance writers aim to find in their battles, boxers do engage in physical combat, and death is not always just a figure of speech.

Any serious consideration of boxing cannot ignore the realities of fighters fighting, bleeding and dying. When facing the sport's dangers, I examine them in tandem with others' writing about them. Professional boxing is a job, and "Health & Safety" addresses the need for related information by scrutinizing how a monumental study of dangers at work deals with fighters' occupational hazards. The death of a boxer doing his work inevitably sparks a search for ways to make the sport safer. However well intentioned some calls for amelioration may be, they can also be misguided, as I argue in "There Are No Easy Answers," a response to a newspaper op-ed piece that draws attention to fans' encouragement of dramatic knockouts and their complicity in the literal death of boxers. In another piece, I address the often overlooked beneficial aspects of boxing.

McIlvanney may also be correct when he says that "anyone who thinks professional boxing can be reduced to a formalized metaphor of violence rather than the real thing ... is deluding himself," but the harsh demands boxing makes on the body, as dangerous as they may truly be, do have undeniable metaphorical possibilities. On stage, singer Henry Rollins is an intensely physical performer. As writer of tour diaries like the one I review in "Rollins on the Road," he perpetuates a lengthy tradition by suggesting similarities between himself and a boxer. He relishes overcoming challenges and enduring. Since he prizes perseverance, it does not surprise when Rollins expresses admiration for Ali – and for Albert Camus, another author who approaches boxing in writerly terms.

Camus, who ranks as a favorite among many who write about boxing, had an amateur boxing background, which makes him one of many writers with actual ring experience.

In *Shadow Box*, George Plimpton recounts his exhibition with then-light heavyweight champion Archie Moore. He also describes other writers' exchanges with boxers. Lord Byron frequently sparred with John Jackson, who was a champion in the 1790s. Paul Gallico inspired Plimpton's foray into "participatory journalism" by getting knocked out by heavyweight champion Jack Dempsey in 1923 and then writing about it. Another reporter, Albert Payson Terhune, had previously sparred with six leading heavyweights and chronicled the outcomes, which included various injuries, in the *New York Evening World*. Ernest Hemingway sparred with Tom Heeney, who fought champion Gene Tunney in 1928, as well as with Tunney himself. Mailer and Budd Schulberg sparred with professionals. A.J. Liebling reportedly had "an excellent left hook when he could move himself into position" and once boxed Philadelphia Jack O'Brien. In "Ahab and Nemesis," Liebling jokes that Camus would have made "a great man to cover the [Rocky Marciano-Archie Moore] fight, but none of the syndicates thought of it." Liebling regards Camus as the kind of literary figure whose writing offers guidance through the difficulties fighters confront.

Whether they hunt for whales or championship titles, men embarking on quests reliably appeal to writers. Then again, ramblers who prefer to follow the meandering, scenic path rather than the most direct route to their destination can also offer narrative potential. Liebling and Herman Melville shared affection for digressions, which I celebrate in a piece on the pair of New Yorkers. The last piece in *The Sweet Science* invokes *Moby-Dick*, offering an example of a literary work providing the essayist with a novel way of writing about boxing, in contrast to the usual turn to the sport for a handy metaphor in writing about something else. (Rotella one ups Liebling in literary gamesmanship by referring to both *Moby-Dick* and "Bartleby the Scrivener" in *Cut Time: An Education at the Fights*.)

Moby-Dick also comes up in another essay not explicitly related to boxing. "Dedicated Writers," a consideration of a certain bookish convention, focuses mainly on a famously combative writer, but mentions Melville's inscription of his novel to Nathaniel Hawthorne, as well as numerous other instances of writers saluting others who influenced, inspired or impressed them. Christopher Hitchens, author of *Letters to a Young Contrarian* and *Slate's* "Fighting Words" columnist, dedicated *God Is Not Great* to one of his contemporaries, a novelist. (It may not be out of place to mention here that the dedicatee displays an interest in brain damage.) Hitchens serves as a useful example of another literary activity in "Write, Repeat," which also discusses a boxing writer (along with several other authors). Appropriately enough, given the essay's examination of repetition, that scribe is none other than Liebling, whom Ward calls the "undefeated heavyweight champion among boxing essayists" and whom I refer to with something like the frequency that Liebling cites Pierce Egan. Liebling and Torres are excellent guides through the world of boxing, and exemplify the complex combination of boxing and writing that ties together these pieces. Tradition in the form of championship status passing by gloved hand directly from one fighter to another intrigues Liebling enough for him to mention the linear progression of title holders in both of his boxing books. Since Liebling's day, the proliferation of sanctioning bodies, each bestowing its own title belts, has complicated the once orderly succession of champions. The sort of cross-generational community he treasured in boxing still operates in a less physical form in the practice of inscribing works to admired authors, the subject of "Dedicated Writers."

Extending another tradition, one dating back to the very beginning of literature, Mailer and Philip Roth show characters dealing with issues of race, age, class, nationality, and gender through their connections with boxing. Even in works not explicitly centered on active fighters or set in boxing environments, the novelists use the sport in ways crucial to the development of both character and plot. They do this both by imagining boxing backgrounds for narrators and protagonists and through poignantly suggestive references to historical boxers. "The Fighting Life" examines the role of boxing in Roth's *The Human Stain* and *Exit Ghost* and Mailer's *Tough Guys Don't Dance.*

A piece of trivia indicates another way boxing and writing can intersect. In 1895, Oscar Wilde sued the Marquis of Queensbury for libel after the marquis called Wilde a sodomite. After losing that case, Wilde was arrested for gross indecency in connection with his love affair with Alfred Douglas, the marquis's son. The rules that, in essence, continue to govern the sport are named for the marquis. (I trace this historical tidbit's connection with Tyson in "Seeing Stars.") "The most important development in the modernization of boxing came with the drafting of the Queensbury Rules in 1865, their publication in 1867, and their wide adoption in 1892," historian Jeffrey T. Sammons writes in *Beyond the Ring*. The Marquis of Queensbury rules introduced leather gloves and instituted one-minute breaks between rounds, which were limited to three minutes. They also increased the authority of referees, who could choose to stop fights when fighters became unable to defend themselves against their opponents. "With the introduction of the referee," Oates asserts in *On Boxing*, "the crudeness of 'The Noble Art' passes over into the relative sophistication of boxing."

Whether in its crude or sophisticated form, "there is only one way to get good at fighting: you have to do it a lot." Rotella says virtually the same thing when describing gyms as "places of repetition." However, that observation does not come from a book about boxing and training such as those I discuss in "A First-Class Sport." Instead, the line comes from

Martin Amis's novel *Money*. While Amis regards masculinity as his natural subject and suffuses his novels with violence, he shows no special interest in clashes where the Queensbury Rules apply. The fictional fights he depicts in *Money* and elsewhere take place in bars or in the street, not on canvas-covered square stages surrounded by ropes.

Anyone who has reviewed several Mailer books, as Amis has, inevitably mentions boxing at some point, however. Amis calls a certain picture of the writer posing in a boxing ring "the second worst photograph of Mailer ever published"; Mailer's worst book jacket image, in Amis's assessment, showed him with a black eye. When writing about actual boxers instead of boxer manqués, Amis gets facts wrong. He calls *The Fight* "an extended waffle on the Ali-Frazier match." There were three Ali-Frazier bouts, and *The Fight* is not about any of them. Instead, Mailer pondered Ali's single fight with George Foreman.

Even if Ali does not enthrall Amis the way he did the author of *The Fight*, I mention the boxer in "Is Martin Amis

Serious?" because of a resemblance I see between the more derisive critics of *The Second Plane* and a degraded version of Ali's style of taunting his opponents. Ali imitators who insult other fighters but lack Ali's charisma fail to recognize that demeaning boxers does nothing to make themselves look good. Similarly, reviewers who resort to *ad hominem* attacks and try to peacock their own syntactical felicities embarrass themselves in their efforts to impugn Amis's seriousness.

Another writer with a deep interest in violence, George Orwell had experience boxing as a school boy. St. Cyprian's, the school Orwell so vividly and scathingly writes about in "Such, Such Were the Joys," encouraged his enthusiasm for boxing and other sports, according to his biographer Jeffrey Meyers. However, that is not my focus in "George & Me." Instead, the suggestion that Orwell might have sexually assaulted a childhood friend prompted me to examine his life – including his involvement as a combatant in the Spanish Civil War – and pay special attention to his relationships with women. The essay describes the process and outcome of my plunge into biographical research. I discuss Orwell's writing and his character, but I mainly recount my response as a reader to distressing news concerning one of my favorite writers.

While "George & Me" makes clear my appreciation of Orwell's way of expressing certain ideas and embodying particular values, "Ink" describes different representatives of worthy qualities. The essay, which combines comments on film and music as well as writing, involves automobiles, though none belonging to Norman Mailer. Among the various topics I consider, I write about a journalist, fight fan, Camus admirer, and member of the Torres and Mailer circle who associates certain admirable properties with a particular prizefighter.

Boxing can infiltrate writers' imagination even when they concentrate on other subjects. In addition to the sport,

Liebling addressed World War II, Southern politicians and French cuisine, but he managed to work boxing into his coverage of those other topics. He inserts a page about shipboard boxing matches organized by soldiers into *Mollie & Other War Pieces*. Visiting Louisiana to profile Governor Earl Long for the *New Yorker* pieces that became *The Earl of Louisiana*, Liebling pays a visit to a New Orleans bar owned by a blind former fighter that he remembered seeing at Madison Square Garden several decades earlier. Amid the reminiscences about food in *Between Meals*, he recalls his own ring exploits as a Sorbonne student in 1926. He believed boxing would help him in his struggle to keep his weight down (a fight he eventually lost). He also remembers seeing George Carpentier box in an exhibition and describes another bout he saw involving a French fighter. "The subject was one which he could not stay away from," according to Plimpton.

Boxing provides Liebling with a frame of reference for assessing the emotional impact of difficult news as well as metaphors for describing the inevitable physical decline men confront with age. When he learns a fellow gastronome is ill, it brings to mind "the moment when [Liebling] first saw Joe Louis draped on the ropes." He likens his friend's attempt to attack a meal with something like his former enthusiasm to "an old fighter who tries a comeback without training for it."

The sport's weight classifications supply Liebling – and me – with an economical way of indicating the size of men not necessarily boxers. When in *Mollie & Other War Pieces* he refers to a soldier as a middleweight, he only means that the man weighs about 160 pounds (like Camus). In "Weight Loss: A Love Story," one of the more personal pieces of mine, I turn to boxing for similar reasons. "To write about boxing is to write about oneself – however elliptically, and unintentionally," Oates says. In this piece, which touches briefly on boxing, I intentionally write about myself. The essay describes how and, far more importantly, why I moved down several weight classes.

With "Fighters & Writers" I again write about myself, as Oates says I must, but I mainly focus on other writers writing about boxing. The essay deals directly with what Rotella calls writers' "constant effort to keep the slippery, naked, near-formless fact of hitting swaddled in layers of sense and form." Inevitably, this means engaging Mailer (as well as Oates). It also means discussing Liebling and Camus. I make a match between two contending camps of thought. In order to assess them, I turn for tips to a former boxing champion who became a writer: José Torres. Neither Mailer nor Oates nor I can settle conclusively which view of the reasons for writers' enduring fascination with the sport has the most merit. Nonetheless, the exchanges between both literary and athletic combatants can be endlessly entertaining.

Thus, *Fighters & Writers* has one subject, not two. It does not group together unconnected articles about writing with pieces about fighting. Instead, the essays and reviews in this collection examine chronicles of conflict or physical and mental challenges (boxing matches are both). Some pieces obliquely involve boxing. Others, such as the title essay, directly engage the issue of the sport's place in many a writer's mind, including my own. Each addresses that "something more" so frequently associated with boxing.

For the world still needs
Its champion as of old, and finds him still.

–Sir Lewis Morris
"The Epic of Hades" (1877)

PART I

ALI & OTHERS

THE ALI ACT

Muhammad Ali's great magic act, like so much of what he did, could not be confined to a single stage. He mastered the trickery of boxing like no one else, using dodges, misdirection and various methods of mentally outmaneuvering boxers in the ring. He also psyched out opponents with his pre-fight antics, manipulating others' emotions to gain an advantage when the physical part of their struggle started. In his truly spectacular feat he played with identity politics as performance art and mesmerized millions. He invoked race, religion, gender and protest in proclaiming who he was but evaded easy classification along any of those lines. Slipperiness inside and outside the ring ensured ongoing public fascination with him. The show started in 1960, when he won Olympic gold, and the spectacle continues to command attention.

José Torres, the former light heavyweight champion, calls a left hook off the jab "a classy lie." To call Ali a classy liar, far from insulting him or questioning the sincerity of his convictions, would acknowledge his athletic prowess and abilities as a performer. A feint, making an opponent expect a punch to land in one place so he will not be prepared when it hits somewhere else, is "an outright lie," Torres explains in *Sting Like a Bee*, a book co-written with Bert Randolph Sugar and contained within the distinguished literary parentheses of a preface by Norman Mailer and an epilogue by Budd Schulberg. "Champions and good fighters are champions and good fighters because they can lie better than the others," according to Torres, and no one was better at it than Ali. Mailer parrots this philosophy of boxing in *The Fight*, his account of Ali's reclaiming of the heavyweight title at 1974's "Rumble in the Jungle" in what was then Zaire. Torres also observes Ali's trickery in his toying with other boxers with insults and outrageous behavior in order to discombobulate them.

Michael Arkush follows in the footsteps both of Torres by focusing on the same timeframe as *Sting Like a Bee* and of Mailer by concentrating on a single bout, but ends up taking a very different journey. For Arkush, the pivotal point in a career with no shortage of dramatic moments was the first of Ali's three bouts with Joe Frazier, which he recounts in *The Fight of the Century*. He concedes that his title does not refer to the best fight in the athletic sense. "There were better fights before March 8, 1971, and there have been better fights since." Instead, it qualifies as "the greatest event in the history of boxing" because of what it signifies. "What separates this fight, what makes it the fight of the century, was what Muhammad Ali and Joe Frazier fought for, and against, and how they fought heroically, and under the kind of pressure, from each other and from society, that no one else, except Joe Louis and Max Schmeling, ever encountered in the ring." Arkush reluctantly allows that the second Louis-Schmeling fight might have claims to the distinction his title confers on Ali-Frazier I but he never seriously entertains the idea that it might carry a heavier symbolic load. A reader unfamiliar with that episode might be confused about why Arkush mentions that fight at all. He does not offer any context; he takes for granted that it has significance that he does not need to explain. That turns out to be his method. He applies it to the main subject, insisting on its resounding importance, but not elucidating the multitude of social and political issues surrounding it.

So what did Frazier and Ali, whom Arkush calls "enshrined symbols of a cultural war, inseparable forever," do to make this particular meeting so meaningful? "While Ali might have been fighting for a 'cause,' so was Frazier," Arkush insists. "His cause was to provide for his wife and children, which was every bit as noble as any principles Muhammad Ali ever espoused." Frazier did represent a bit more than a hard-working man's willingness to support his family, including an unflagging work ethic, tenacity and dedication. His trainer worried he trained too hard. "Frazier often wanted to go that one extra round with his sparring partners and never held anything back." The determined preparation other athletes might regard as drudgery, Frazier took to with enthusiasm. He happily pushed the rock to the top of the mountain each day because he liked his job. "Few prizefighters in history have derived as much pure enjoyment from demolishing the body and spirit of another living creature as Smokin' Joe Frazier did," says Arkush. In the lead-up to his fight with Ali, Frazier, against his will, became another sort of symbol. Ali called Frazier an Uncle Tom, among other insults. Frazier's friendliness with Philadelphia's police commissioner, Frank Rizzo – "an enemy to many African Americans," as Arkush notes (twice) – did not make him popular in his adopted city. Frazier, who previously had not been a polarizing figure, became the fighter associated with the "white Establishment," largely because of Ali's efforts. "Ali claimed that he was fighting for a cause while Frazier was fighting for a check, and that Frazier was too ugly and too dumb to be the heavyweight champion."

So what was Ali's cause? Oddly, given the rich vein of symbolism that numerous other writers have mined, Arkush is essentially silent about the meaning of Muhammad Ali. Ali claimed that black people around the world identified with him, but Arkush does not even try to explain how this came to be. Instead, he traces Ali's prominence to his defiant 1967 decision to refuse induction into the United States Armed Forces, after which he was stripped of his title as heavyweight champion and barred from boxing for three and a half years. (Frazier became the official champion during Ali's exile).

Denounced as unpatriotic, he was sentenced to five years in prison, but remained free on bail until the Supreme Court in 1971 overturned his conviction for violating the Selective Service Act. Opponents of the Vietnam War found a hero in the person who said, "Man, I ain't got no quarrel with them Vietcong." Virtually no one in the country was neutral about Ali in the late 1960s, according to Arkush.

Undeniably, though, Ali was much more than just America's "most famous draft dodger," as Arkush dubs him. While Arkush acknowledges that the fight had a "racial component," he shies away from examining it in any detail. Ali struggled "to convince blacks that 'black is beautiful,'" according to Torres. Thomas Hauser, the author of an Ali biography that Joyce Carol Oates says "would appear to be definitive, and is certainly exhaustive" as well as multiple other books on the boxer, writes in one of them that "the experience of being black changed because of Muhammad Ali." Tennis star Arthur Ashe, for instance, said Ali "helped give an entire people a belief in themselves and the will to make themselves better." This had definite political results. "One of the reasons the civil rights movement went forward was that black people were able to overcome their fear," in the assessment of Bryant Gumbel, who believes that, "for many black Americans, that came from watching Muhammad Ali. He simply refused to be afraid. And being that way, he gave other people courage."

Ali's praise of his physical appearance had implications involving gender as well as race, as Mike Marqusee observes in *Redemption Song: Muhammad Ali and the Spirit of the Sixties*. When Ali boasted, "I'm too beautiful to be a fighter," he broke "the taboo against exhibitions of male vanity," writes Marqusee. "He was not only 'the Greatest' but 'the prettiest,' a superlative usually associated with female attractiveness.... [T]he feminine side of this master pugilist was always an essential element of his popular chemistry." Marqusee suggests that Ali's challenging assumptions about black and male "physicality" helped him challenge other conventions as well.

Upending concepts of race and gender and defying authority by refusing to go to war were not Ali's only high-profile transgression or even the main reasons for his controversial fame. Soon after becoming the heavyweight champion of the world in 1964 by upsetting Sonny Liston, Cassius Clay revealed his new identity as Muhammad Ali and affiliation with Elijah Muhammad, Malcolm X and the Nation of Islam, an organization very much at odds not only with mainstream religions but also with the Civil Rights movement. "We who follow the teachings of Elijah Muhammad don't want to force integrate," Ali explained. "Integration is wrong. We don't want to live with the white man; that's all." Indeed, he explicitly distinguished himself from Civil Rights activists. When he announced his conversion, he referred to the deadly 1963 bombing of a church in Birmingham, Alabama. "I ain't no Christian," he said. "I can't be when I see all the colored people fighting for forced integration get blowed up."

In addition to a racial program sinisterly in sync with that of the Ku Klux Klan, the outfit Ali joined also featured a cosmology straight out of a science fiction tale. The Original Man, a black man who became known as Allah, created the universe and the black race. Trillions of years later, an evil scientist with an exceptionally big head known as Mr. Yacub engineered a race of small-brained "white devils," who subsequently were civilized by Moses and went on to subjugate others. As David Remnick puts it in *King of the World: Muhammad Ali and the Rise of an American Hero*:

> Eventually the whites came to be dominant, first in Europe, then in the New World, where they imported slaves from Africa and treated them brutally – force-feeding them swine and Christianity, making them lose touch with the

radiant civilization of their ancestors, the Original Men.

In addition to telling a story about where the world and everyone in it came from, the Nation of Islam also concocted one about the future, which would see the arrival of a large round spacecraft called the Mother Plane. A week or so before the ultimate retribution of Allah, the ship would drop directions for the faithful to follow in order to escape the imminent attack on the earth. Hundreds of planes would then take off from the Mother Plane and destroy the planet with bombs. Eventually, the righteous black survivors would construct a new civilization free of Yacub's fiends.

Ali's commitment to a black separatist religion complicated efforts to see him as an advocate of equal rights. White Christians were not the only people who found the Nation of Islam disturbing. Arthur Ashe may have appreciated Ali's power to inspire, but he rejected his beliefs. "I never went along with the pronouncements of Elijah Muhammad that the white man was the devil and blacks should be striving for separate development; a sort of American apartheid.... It was a racist ideology, and I didn't like it." Joe Louis, who joined the military as heavyweight champion, also disapproved of Ali's affiliation with the Nation of Islam. "I'm against Black Muslims. I've always believed that every man is my brother. Clay will earn the public's hatred because of his connections with the Black Muslims. The things they preach are just the opposite of what we believe. The heavyweight champion should be the champion of all people." The decision to continue calling him Clay, as Louis, members of Frazier's camp and most in the press did, reflected a discomfort with the bizarre and frightening ideas his Muslim name represented. Torres, who did not condemn Ali, did see that "the fears whites felt toward the Black Muslims were not altogether paranoid" and admits that when he, "part black and a Puerto Rican," visited a mosque with Ali he "wasn't too comfortable" with what the minister said. Torres believes Ali became the heavyweight champion the first time by adeptly playing mental games. He does not suggest that allegiance to the Nation of Islam was a ploy to unsettle others, but he does think it had that effect. "Sonny Liston had lost both of his fights with Ali for the same reason: he was psyched out in both fights…. In the first, because initially he was completely frustrated, and then became discouraged; in the second, Sonny Liston feared Muhammad Ali. And, even more, he feared the Black Muslims." If this is so, religion and ring savvy cannot be separated when considering the Ali phenomenon.

Ali's adherence to the Nation of Islam until Elijah Muhammad's death in 1975 reveals something of the boxer's personality. Even while advocating racial separatism, he surrounded himself with white people, including his trainer, Angelo Dundee, and his physician, Ferdie Pacheco, who believed what his patient really liked about the group was its strength and ability to strike fear in others. Ali reserved his most denigrating comments about his opponents' appearance and intelligence for other black fighters. Ali did not convert to orthodox Islam and express more inclusive ideas about race until ten years after the assassination of former fellow-thinker and friend Malcolm X.

Astonishingly, Arkush ignores almost all of this. He barely mentions Ali's religion. Though he dutifully notes the boxer's claim to be exempt from military service "as a minister of the religion of Islam" and the Supreme Court's determination four years later that his religious beliefs were indeed sincerely held, Arkush says nothing of what those beliefs were. He mentions the Nation of Islam only in passing, reporting the fighter's public statement of membership after first beating Liston. He refers to Ali's short suspension from the group because of its leader's displeasure over comments Ali made about wanting to return to the sport for financial reasons. That's it. Arkush briefly glances at Martin Luther King Jr.'s "dream of a color-blind America" but does not try to reconcile the fighter's views at that time with King's vision. He only mentions King because he and the Georgia state senator who helped Ali obtain a boxing license for his first post-exile fight in 1970 graduated from the same college. He has nothing to say about Malcolm X.

Ignoring major parts of his legendary subject's story, Arkush covers territory extensively explored by others. His thesis can be found in the biography that appeared seventeen years earlier. In 1991's *Muhammad Ali: His Life and Times*, Hauser writes: "The first Ali-Frazier fight was the biggest event in the history of boxing. Due to changes in the industry, there have been subsequent fights that generated more revenue, but no fight ever transcended boxing as Ali-Frazier I did throughout the world." Arkush ends *The Fight of the Century* with short summaries of what later happened to characters who played small roles in the Ali-Frazier drama. By presenting brief encapsulations of the sad fates of fighters, Arkush makes that same move Mark Kram does in the concluding chapter of *Ghosts of Manila*, his consideration of Ali and Frazier's trilogy of bouts. Even with fight-related marginalia, Arkush mimics his predecessors. He says Frazier's trainer, Yank Durham, "often used the first person when talking to the press about his fighter," echoing a line by A.J. Liebling, the *New Yorker* scribe whose boxing essays were collected in *The Sweet Science* and *A Neutral Corner*. In one called "Poet and Pedagogue" about none other than Cassius Clay (as he was still then known), Liebling mentions that "the substitution of the first for the third person in conversation is managerial usage." (He goes on to joke that the manager is sure to "resubstitute [the boxer] for himself in the actual fight.") Arkush also refers to "the esteemed poet T.S. Ali," giving this example of his work in rhyme: "Frazier will catch hell. From the start of the bell. Then we'll jump out. And take on Howard Cosell." (Of the boxer's literary endeavors, Mailer writes, "For Ali to compose a few words of real poetry would be equal to an intellectual throwing a good punch.") Liebling, writing forty six years earlier than Arkush, records verse Clay spoke while doing sit ups, noting that the boxer "is the only poet in America who can recite this way. I would like to see T.S. Eliot try."

Arkush appears to do what others have already done, only less. Without the boxing experience of Torres, he cannot impart an insider's insight into the art and skill of the sport. He does not try to cover all the angles the way Hauser does in his biography and subsequent works. (Unlike Hauser, Arkush did not interview either Ali or Frazier.) He glosses over major elements of Ali's background and public persona by disregarding his religion. "By focusing on Ali's ring exploits and his refusal to serve in Vietnam, while at the same time covering up the true nature of Nation of Islam doctrine, the current keepers of Ali's legacy are losing sight of why he so enthralled and enraged segments of American society," Hauser wrote a few years before *The Fight of the Century* appeared in 2008. Arkush does exactly what Hauser condemns. Further, he does not bring the verbal flair or wit of a Liebling to what he does say.

A specialty within the field of Ali studies is the reassessment, but Arkush neither offers a new way of viewing Ali-Frazier I nor challenges popular views of the fighters. In 2005's *The Lost Legacy of Muhammad Ali*, Hauser presents what he regards as the real meaning and continued relevance of Ali's life. He laments what he calls the "sanitization" of Ali, believing the full complexity of the famous figure's history has become obscured. He believes Ali's greatness can only be appreciated by understanding his total struggle and the distance he traveled since first attaining notoriety. Hauser sees Ali as possessing vital importance – "to many, he was the ultimate symbol of black pride and black resistance to an unjust social order" – that is in danger of being diminished as he becomes a generic representative of greatness suitable for commercial exploitation in advertisements for athletic shoes, computers and the like. Marqusee too wants to reclaim the figure from the forces that "homogenized and repackaged [him] for sale in an ever-burgeoning marketplace for cultural commodities." He worries that the "icon" has grown "irresistible to capitalism," which has softened his image in order to make him a flexible pitchman. "Ali continues to mean different things to different people," Marqusee grants. However, "the various meanings are by no means all compatible," and he thinks he has located his true significance as a sort of post-national activist. Like Hauser, he says the changes in Ali's outlook are important, but his fearlessly acting on since-disregarded beliefs continues to resonate. "Ali's embrace of an alternative nationality, in the form of the Nation of Islam, evolved under the pressure of events into a humanist internationalism, a sense of responsibility to the poor and powerless of all nations."

When Clay became Ali, he said, "I don't have to be what you want me to be. I'm free to be what I want," and this defiant expression of nonconformity enamors him to those, like Marqusee, who want to claim Ali for leftist causes, despite what he chose to be when he spoke those words. Even though Marqusee refers to this as a "declaration of independence," he adamantly insists that Ali's was not merely fulfilling a national paradigm. "America...wants to embrace Muhammad Ali and even convert him into a symbol of national identity.... [But] what makes Ali a role model is precisely his rejection of American national identity in favor of a broader, transnational sense of selfhood and social responsibility." Marqusee regards as virtuous what detractors earlier deemed unpatriotic. Arkush does not set out to correct misunderstandings or to make such grandiloquent claims.

Star gazers create constellations in the celebrity firmament by connecting certain bright and shiny points. Hauser draws a line from Ali to King; Remnick between him

and Malcolm X. Hauser calls Ali "a living embodiment" of
King's message that "all people are deserving of love."
Remnick describes Malcolm X in the very terms usually used
with Ali: "He became a symbol of uncompromising strength,
authenticity, and virility." Remnick also argues that in certain
respects Ali followed Malcolm's path both by joining the
Nation of Islam as "a gesture of self-assertion and racial
solidarity" and by later becoming "more inclusive in his
rhetoric and more devout." Marqusee seems to regard Ali as a
sort of Che Guevara, the archetypical rebel pathetically
reduced to a content-free T-shirt icon.

Mark Kram has no patience for any of this. He wrote
Ghosts of Manila as "a corrective to the years of stenography
that have produced the Ali legend." He believes that myth
making machinery transported a person with uncommon
athletic ability into an absurd counterfactual fantasyland. "He
has been celebrated for the wrong reasons and has been
interpreted by an increasingly uninformed generation of
media that was barely born at the height of his career." He
forcefully rejects efforts to put Ali in the same category of
those with real worldly significance. Views like those of
Hauser and Marqusee are anathema to Kram, who complains
that

> countless hagiographers never tire of trying to
> persuade us that he ranked second only to Martin
> Luther King, but have no compelling argument with
> which to support that claim. Ali was no more a
> social force than Frank Sinatra. Nor was he
> especially complex, unless you happen to view
> instant contradiction of utterance as deep. The
> politically fashionable clung to his racial invective as
> if it were the wisdom of a seer. Today, such are the
> times, he would be looked upon as a contaminant, a
> chronic user of hate language and a sexual
> profligate.

Hauser may sincerely believe that Ali "was the living embodiment of the proposition that principles matter" and that "whether or not people liked the racial component of Ali's views, there was respect for the fact that he had stood by them," but this is nonsense to Kram, who thinks he has gotten to the core of the man and found little there. The supposedly principled stand against the draft does not impress him. "The sad truth was that Ali was played like a harp by the Muslims, a daft cult with a long record of draft dodging from Elijah (who went to prison) on down." He insists that the media got Ali wrong in the 1960s and 1970s and continued to confuse matters even after switching from criticism to praise. "The press coverage of Ali (seldom called by that name) and his troubles was as misguided and excessive as the throwing of flowers in his path today." Kram also questions Ali's intelligence and the incisiveness of his vaunted wit: "Seldom has a public figure of such superficial depth been more wrongly perceived – by the right and the left." Those cheering or booing Ali generally agree that his lighting of the Olympic flame in Atlanta in 1996 was another key development in the Ali saga. Visibly struggling with the symptoms of Parkinson's syndrome to make a symbolic gesture in the city where he resumed his boxing career twenty six years before, Ali provided yet another instance of an uncanny ability to overcome adversity. Even this, though, can be argued about. Where Hauser saw "a glorious moment," Kram sensed just more "sentimentality" pouring down on an undeserving sports figure. Hauser and Marqusee also dislike what Hauser calls corporate America's "rediscovery" of Ali after Atlanta.

Arkush refuses to join these debates. He offers little new information and no reappraisal of the still-controversial figure. As Marqusee asks, "What possible justification can there be for adding yet more to the millions of words already in print on the subject of Muhammad Ali?" Arkush's reasons are less earnest than Hauser's, less prickly and contrarian than Kram's and less tendentious than Marqusee's. He does not ponder the "social implications" he says eager fans lining up for fight tickets huddled together to discuss. He too claims Ali ascended to the status of an icon at the 1996 Summer Games, but does not say what he represented.

Ultimately, *The Fight of the Century* is a study of spectacle-making and the nature of celebrity, though Arkush does not explicitly present it this way. By stripping away – or ignoring – so much of the Ali mystique, Arkush does not aim to get behind the hype to the real history. Instead, he recognizes that with Ali the hype is the history. There is no getting past the façade to the real figure when the two are indivisible. Ali is the carefully constructed public image and not just an astonishingly talented athlete who for three and a half years could not compete in his sport. Arkush says a promoter of the fight "wisely recognized that this was a spectacle more than a sporting contest and that every decision must be viewed in that context." This is precisely how Arkush views it. Implicitly arguing that what confers significance is public interest, he attends to measurements of the event as popular entertainment. He reports how much the boxers were paid ($2.5 million each), the number of people who saw the fight via closed-circuit television broadcasts (an estimated 300 million), the number of people in attendance at Madison Square Garden (20,455) and the celebrities among them (such as Gene Kelly, Woody Allen, Michael Caine, Diana Ross, Edward Kennedy and Joe Namath). The traffic disruptions caused by taxis and limousines dropping off passengers interest Arkush, as do the prices scalpers charged for tickets (three or four times face value if not more). The number of countries (26) from which journalists came to the fight points to its stature as a spectacle, as does the prominence of some of those who covered it. Mailer wrote about it for *Life,* and that social force Frank Sinatra served as the magazine's photographer. Schulberg, author of the novel *The Harder They*

Fall and the screenplay *On the Waterfront*, reported it for *Playboy*.

Arkush, Rush Limbaugh's unauthorized biographer, admires Ali's abilities to attract and sustain attention through his performances. Before the fight with Frazier, "Ali played his part magnificently. Nobody in the history of boxing – of any sport – was a more creative and unabashed self-promoter." Arkush is hardly alone in noticing this, but, again, he does not try to attach any overarching significance to Ali's superb skill. Self-promotion is self-justifying. For Marqusee, Ali's routines outside the ring had major cultural impact: "Of course, the swagger, the bragging, the manic competitive zeal had always been part of the subculture of big-time sports; but it was Cassius Clay who brought these qualities out of hiding and fashioned them into a saleable image.... The braggadocio which perplexed so many was a type of playground foolery orchestrated for the modern media circus." For cranky Kram, such shenanigans amount to no more than "brainless exhibitionism" that subsequently became all too common among athletes. But for Arkush, what matters is not what they signify or their lingering influence. What matters is that they worked. They made people willing to pay money to see Ali do his thing.

Instead of being an emblem of black pride, the embodiment of rebellion or the surest sign of capitalism's capacity to transform almost anything into a commodity, Ali for Arkush is above all a celebrity, the star of a show that received unprecedented hype. "My first impression of Cassius Clay was of someone with an incredibly versatile personality," Hauser quotes Alex Haley as recalling. "You never knew quite where he was in psychic posture. He was almost like that shell game, with a pea and three shells. You know; which shell is the pea under? But he had a belief in himself and conviction far stronger than anybody dreamed he would." Uninterested in those convictions, Arkush focuses on the

game and its master player. The versatility Haley noted makes
the Ali performance possible. He might have insisted that he
did not have to be what others wanted him to be, but over the
course of almost fifty years of fame he proved capable of
allowing others to see in him whatever it was they wanted to
see. Over time, and after years of his frequent proclamations
of his own greatness, Ali's name became synonymous with
that word.

Ali's reputation for greatness spurred congress to pass a
law named after him, though few believe it lives up to the
implied promise of the association with the hero. The
Muhammad Ali Boxing Reform Act, enacted in 2000,
attempted to fix some of boxing's notoriously corrupt
business practices, focusing on issues like promotional
contracts and sanctioning organizations' systems for rating
fighters. Hauser, who in addition to chronicling the exploits
and preserving the image of Ali has written extensively on
boxing regulation and related legislation, said the act "leaves a
lot to be desired" but was "a step in the right direction."
Trainer and television analyst Teddy Atlas was more critical
and used popular perceptions of its namesake to make his
point. A couple years after the bill was passed, in an interview
about the Ali Act and other reform efforts, Atlas remarked
that while he knows the name was chosen so people would
think that, like Ali, the law must be good, he saw it differently.
The act made him think of the fighter late in his career
"laying on the ropes, doing nothing." Atlas summed up the
law as "a lot of shuffle, not enough punching, too much rope-
a-dope." With Ali, Atlas implies, appearances conceal what's
actually going on. Arkush offers a telling anecdote involving
Ali's artifice in 1971. For his fight with Frazier, Ali picked
showy white shoes with red tassels. He wore them, he said,
"so that the judges can be impressed when I'm dancing –
makes me look like I'm going faster." Where some might see
a fraud, others see a showman, while still others really believe
what they think they are seeing. Even such a straightforward

matter as the outcome the fight settled nothing. Ali lost. Yet "considering the obstacles," Arkush says, "it was one of Ali's greatest nights in the ring. Even in defeat, he, too, was a winner." Arkush does not try to reconcile the incompatible meanings surrounding Ali. He quietly accepts that there is no one meaning beyond the versatile persona that Ali so skillfully shaped to always look like a winner.

In order to do this, Ali moved back and forth between public remembering and forgetting. As Remnick writes: "Everything about the Nation of Islam that was once so threatening or obscure – the separatist rhetoric that was greeted so heartily by the KKK, the talk of 'big-headed' Yacub and mysterious spaceships – all that, for Ali, has been forgotten long ago." Even in the early acts of his show, he was able to dance among competing historical forces, allowing white college students to forget about his hostile separatist beliefs and hold onto his opposition to the Vietnam War, for example, or letting Civil Rights activists take him as a symbol of a movement whose aims he vocally rejected. Whatever they might ultimately mean, these are impressive tricks, and Ali pulled them off over and over again.

SEEING STARS

Boxing's chroniclers write as though athletic contests can reveal key aspects of the culture at large. But boxing in particular, they generally insist, is more than just fighting governed by the Marquis of Queensbury rules. Boxing says something about race, wealth, poverty, masculinity, religion and violence in ways that other sports do not, and when the focus comes down to superhuman spectacles like Mike Tyson and Muhammad Ali, the case seems plausible not despite but because of the contrast between the two men.

Ali mesmerized with a studied ambiguity; his quickness and bantering personality hid his power and determination in the ring. Outside the ring he took stands on major issues, ascending in the eyes of many from pariah to beloved symbol of courage. Tyson's strength and focus inside the ring were not in the least ambiguous, and his boorishness and crudity outside of it took his fame in the opposite direction. From looking like an indestructible prospect headed for certain greatness, Tyson's shattered star soon shined only for insatiable connoisseurs of schadenfreude, while Ali's only got brighter over time. Two films, especially when seen together, spark reflections not only on these diverging personal narratives, but on boxing and the "big issues" it claims to reflect.

In the documentary *Tyson*, director James Toback aims to add to the story of the boxer's messy life by concentrating on the sensitivity and thoughtfulness not usually associated with the former "baddest man on the planet." The film doesn't downplay Tyson's shabby and criminal behavior – though the fighter denies committing the rape for which he was convicted – but it permits the ex-heavyweight champion to express his purportedly hard-won maturity and the insights gained from introspection.

Toback doesn't attempt an exhaustive history. Instead, he compiles a case study of celebrity gone awry. Tyson, the sole speaker in the documentary, gives an ambitious if somewhat unconvincing performance. Tyson chokes up and nears tears when recalling Cus D'Amato, his boxing trainer and manager. Tyson was a fat, essentially parentless kid, often in trouble with the law, who found in D'Amato the first person he could trust and love. D'Amato was already known for being the upstate New York boxing trainer and manager who, three decades earlier, helped Floyd Patterson become the youngest heavyweight champion of his time. D'Amato spied in Tyson a late-in-life shot at repeating the feat. D'Amato not only worked with Tyson on physical conditioning; he also cultivated the mental component he believed was the principal part of boxing.

Indeed, Tyson pays his debt to D'Amato by proclaiming himself a master of "the art of skullduggery." He thinks he won many of his fights by intimidating his opponents before the bout ever began. Having early on established the crushing power of his punches, Tyson for later matches would emerge from his dressing room not sheathed in a showy silk robe like other boxers but as a sweating destroyer in black trunks eager to go to work. Stalking around the ring, intently staring down the other man, he sought to assert the terror of his own personality. Tyson remembers living in constant fear as a child in the "horrific" Brownsville section of Brooklyn, but feeling fright subside the closer he stepped to a boxing ring. He enjoyed outsmarting others as a criminal, and he found application for that skill in boxing. As a boxer, he prevailed by causing in other fighters the very fear he struggled to squelch in himself.

Tyson describes the arc of his life as first the gaining of this confidence he needed to become the heavyweight champion and then the gradual loss of that confidence as he fell into a mess of personal turmoil. Though he came to possess unshakable confidence in his talent, the very lessening of the fear that spurred his success then undermined his ability to sustain it. So certain of his invincibility was he that he trained less and less as time passed.

Tyson attributes the disastrous course of his boxing career to events outside the ring, however. Just as he repeats his mentor's theories about the psychology of fighting, he seems to mouth lines he learned in rehab when he claims to take responsibility for his poor choices and behavior. But at the same time he repeatedly finds ways to suggests that events beyond his control were the real causes of such choices.

Perhaps there is some truth here. D'Amato's death, coming soon before Tyson reached the pinnacle of his career, shook his confidence. The public breakdown of his brief marriage to the actress Robin Givens weakened it further. Tyson judged the best punch he ever threw to be the one that bounced Givens off every wall in the room, according to *Fire & Fear: The Inside Story of Mike Tyson*, a 1989 biography by José Torres, a D'Amato trainee and former light heavyweight champion. (In revealing contrast, George Foreman, in director Pete McCormack's *Facing Ali*, names Ali the greatest fighter he ever fought because of a punch *not* thrown—of which more below.)

Tyson's 1992 rape conviction further damaged his always-fragile mental state. Anger animates the often subdued speaker when he disparages his accuser, beauty queen Desiree Washington, "that wretched swine of a woman." He hurls similarly spiteful insults at one of the "leeches" he blames for his financial ruin, the "wretched, slimy, reptilian" boxing promoter Don King, whom he accuses of bilking him of millions of dollars.

The film never gets to the bottom of such accusations, because it can't. But it does show that King recognized precisely what Tyson also realized: No one sells tickets like Mike Tyson. The ex-boxer knows what to say to get attention, whether this means saying calculatedly shocking things—such as his proclaimed wish to devour Lennox Lewis's children, or his description of visualizing punching through to the backs of other boxers' heads—or therapeutic confessions suitable for daytime talk shows, as when he admits to heavy drug use, laments his divorces and describes his financial troubles.

Ironically, Tyson's greatest fear as a youngster was to be publicly, humiliatingly beaten up. His irreversible decline as a fighter involves precisely that: the embarrassing loss of his title to underdog James "Buster" Douglas, his disqualification after biting off part of Evander Holyfield's ear, his dismantlement at the hands of Lewis (whose leg Tyson bit at a press conference), and his risible performances against journeymen he would have dispatched in seconds during the days when he inspired the right balance of fear in others and confidence in himself. In an article reprinted in her 2009 collection *One Ring Circus*, Katherine Dunn defended Tyson's dental maneuver in the 1997 Holyfield fight, and in the film, Tyson echoes her argument that the other boxer's repeated head butts were the real, overlooked problem. (In October 2009, Tyson appeared on *Oprah* and admitted he felt no guilt at the time about the incident from roughly a dozen years earlier. On a return visit with Holyfield, Tyson attempted something resembling amends by telling the "beautiful guy" at his side that it had been "a pleasure passing through life being acquainted with you." Holyfield, as if reading from a generic script, said he hoped children learned something about conflict resolution.)

For all his excuse-making, Tyson desperately wants the fame he can't handle. Even decades after his discovery that he was known all over the world, he sounds startled by it. He lists places he went before parole limitations interfered with his travels, speaking of them as achievements no less important than the big fights he won. He knows that he is widely viewed as "a bad black man," in contrast to the vocally Christian, and therefore "good," Holyfield, but he is never reconciled to his role, expecting fans to distinguish between his professional "show" persona and who he really is as a man.

Race does arise in *Tyson*. When he was welcomed into the D'Amato household, he thought about how he could "rob these white folks." In a tirade at a media event, he says a white heckler could never understand or survive his world. Religion surfaces too, as when Tyson describes becoming a militant Muslim while incarcerated, only to find that he didn't really understand Islam. More than race or religion, however, Tyson mostly enjoys musing on sex and his desire to dominate powerful women.

Toback presents Tyson the monologist alternately with bright sun shining through windows behind him or in a darkened room, as if to hint at the extremes of his subject's psyche. He occasionally shoots the reflective pugilist staring off at the ocean, as if to suggest his depth. Toback also splits the screen into multiple views of Tyson's face (or parts of it), indicating visually the fractured state of the fighter's soul. Toback seeks cinematic expression of an idea voiced two decades earlier, in *Fire & Fear*, where Torres wonders if "there were really two Tysons," one "sensitive and compassionate" and another who "enjoyed the sight of pain and hurt in others." If these obvious and intrusive cues grow tedious, they provide some relief from the unceasing self-exposure of a man who veers between self-awareness and delusion.

Toback has Tyson read part of Oscar Wilde's poem "The Ballad of Reading Gaol," presumably because crime and punishment make up part of the boxer's personal province. (Wilde's own legal troubles involved his relationship with the son of the marquis after whom modern-day boxing's rules are named, which Tyson, a dedicated student of the sport's history, surely knows.) However, another author, Cyril Connolly, more accurately sums up the boxer's biography. Tyson's explosive start as a professional—beating 25 of his first 27 opponents inside the distance, 15 of them by way of first-round knockouts, before winning the World Boxing Council belt from Trevor Berbick at age twenty and proceeding to capture other organizations' belts to become the undisputed champion—persuaded many that he'd hold his title much longer than the three years he did. As Connolly says, "whom the gods wish to destroy they first call promising."

With Muhammad Ali, observers were far less optimistic—at least at the beginning. A.J. Liebling, the dean of boxing writers, judged Cassius Clay's gold medal-winning performance at the 1960 Olympics "attractive but not probative." He said Clay, as Ali was then known, "had a skittering style, like a pebble over water" and lacked punching power. Even after Clay turned professional and beat a dozen and half opponents, Liebling still wondered if the boxer would ever learn to hit harder. Sonny Liston joked that Clay ought to be arrested for impersonating a prizefighter.

Of course, that was before Liston lost to him—twice. Going into his first fight for the title against Liston, Clay was a seven-to-one underdog (not as prohibitive as the 42-to-1 odds against Buster Douglas, but still steep). Both sports writers and the boxing commissioners expected Liston, a fighter with Tyson-like style and temperament, to thoroughly thrash the challenger. Clay shocked the experts, rather than merely living up to expectations as Tyson did in his initial quest for the heavyweight crown.

Liebling did not live to see Clay transform into Ali and become reviled as a draft-dodging member of the separatist Nation of Islam. Nor did the *New Yorker* writer see Ali's refusal to fight in the Vietnam War (because, he famously said, no Vietcong ever called him "nigger") come to look like a principled stand, and his three-and-a-half year suspension from boxing (which lasted roughly as long as Tyson's prison term) become popularly perceived as unjust. "To think about Ali is to think about race," according to Gerald Early, author of *The Culture of Bruising: Essays on Prizefighting, Literature, and Modern American Culture* and the editor of *The Muhammad Ali Reader*. The man Liebling dubbed "the heavyweight poet from Louisville" became the embodiment of the Civil Rights movement despite what he actually advocated. Changes in popular attitudes toward Ali, and changes in Ali's outlook, such as his embrace of a de-radicalized version of Islam, may truly reflect changes in the nation's thinking about race.

For all Liebling's doubts, Ali did develop a punch strong enough to put supposedly invincible George Foreman on the canvas in Zaire in the famous 1974 "Rumble in the Jungle." That triumph, in which Ali reclaimed his illegitimately denied title, along with his status as a figure of global fascination, are examined in Leon Gast's Academy Award-winning documentary, *When We Were Kings*. Gast's film, which mostly sidesteps Ali's more incendiary statements, was released soon after a Parkinson's-afflicted Ali made a poignant appearance at the 1996 Olympics to reignite the torch, as well as his fame.

The fire of the latter continues to burn, as admirers tend to it. *Facing Ali*, produced in association with Muhammad Ali Enterprises and based on a 2003 book by Stephen Brunt, is a video love letter to the boxer who awed even those opponents who beat him. Both it and *Tyson* allow boxers to tell their own stories, but there the similarities between the two movies end. A straightforward documentary without attention-grabbing editing tricks, *Facing Ali* speeds through obligatory mentions of controversies to concentrate on Ali the performer. If *Tyson* enters the fighter's head in search of previously unseen and unsuspected complexity, *Facing Ali* looks from the outside at the phenomenon, offers a streamlined hagiography of a personification of fame, and celebrates Ali's impact on others. Men he fought reflect on Ali's athletic prowess, his charismatic personality and his effect on them.

Most sound star-struck. Ken Norton, who broke Ali's jaw in a 1973 bout, says: "To be in the same ring with this man called Muhammad was to me an honor, a life saver, career saver and I can't thank him enough for giving me the chance." Norton had marital and financial troubles; he saw fighting Ali as a means of feeding and clothing his son and having "a chance at a life, period." Later a car accident left Norton paralyzed for years. He was told that, while comatose, he nonetheless responded when Ali visited him in the hospital. Norton is shown walking with a cane and is one of several boxers in *Facing Ali* whose slurred or mumbled words are rendered onscreen. Clips of the young, verbally dexterous Ali are shown; the older Ali appears only briefly, and silently.

Larry Holmes, an Ali sparring partner who succeeded him as heavyweight champion, declares: "I love him like a brother and like a guy that's a celebrity." He explains that "Ali was one of those guys that made you feel good about yourself." Foreman calls him "a hero to the world." Leon Spinks—whose story of growing up brutally poor, learning to protect himself from bullies, becoming a young champion, and having drug-related problems prefigures Tyson's—deposed his avowed idol in their first 1978 fight. After handing back the title belt later the same year, Spinks thanked Ali because "there's only one Ali." Earnie Shavers says fighting Ali changed his life. "Just his name's got magic, if you do well with him."

Even those whose comments on Ali amount to more than unalloyed adulation testify to his uniqueness. *Pace* Larry Holmes, Ali didn't make Joe Frazier feel good. Frazier never stopped resenting Ali for calling him an Uncle Tom. Even so, he ends up calling Ali a great guy. Ron Lyle insists on Ali's importance outside the ring, but acknowledges that no one would seek his opinion if he hadn't met Ali inside one. Lyle believes Ali "meant a lot to the black community, and he means a lot today," and he draws a connection between Ali and Malcolm X. Lyle was devastated when the referee stopped his 1975 fight against Ali, which he thought he was winning, because it was his "moment." Ali's last fight (which *Facing Ali* ignores) was a loss to Trevor Berbick in 1981. Tyson, in his film, recounts that Ali told him to beat Berbick for his sake. He also recalls D'Amato telling him that Ali's personality was what made him a great fighter. Tyson didn't understand the remark at the time.

If Tyson did eventually discover what D'Amato meant, he either didn't or couldn't follow Ali's example of image cultivation. Tyson never developed the media-savvy of his predecessor, who could be amusing and likable even when insulting people. This may have been in part because the forces shaping the fighters were so dissimilar. "You've got to want to get out of the environment you're in," says Henry Cooper in *Facing Ali* of the struggle to exit poverty. "That's what motivates a fighter." However, Ali's less tumultuous upbringing sets him apart. Ali came from a middle-class background and a loving family—far different circumstances than the vicious poverty and domestic chaos that forged Tyson and most other boxers. While Ali could play the fierce critic and the charming clown simultaneously, Tyson made his living by being, or at least seeming, a menace, a threat and a misfit.

"A boxing match is like a cowboy movie," said Sonny Liston. "There's got to be good guys, and there's got to be bad guys." The ex-convict thought he could wear only the black hat. Movies about Ali show that, in boxing, the same man can play both parts and appeal to a wide audience. Ali perfected the capacity for ceaseless reinvention. Tyson may have, like Ali, become immediately recognizable around the world, but with his more limited style of celebrity, he only enamors those who deem unrelenting ugliness more authentic than the ability to change. While Toback doesn't try to recast Tyson as a glorious giant in the Ali mold, he does try to help the fighter expand his range. Ali established his movie-star bona fides well before retirement. "What a Hollywood ending," George Chuvalo says in *Facing Ali* regarding the upset Ali pulled off in Zaire (where, arm cocked as Foreman starting falling, Ali refrained from throwing an unnecessary additional punch). "Have you ever seen anything more Hollywood than that?"

THE CINDERELLA MAN FAIRYTALE

James J. Braddock was a hero of his times, but not a hero for all times. It takes nothing away from the former world heavyweight champion to point out that the fairy-tale elements of the Cinderella Man's life story were particularly resonant during the Depression, when he overcame great odds to achieve success. Boxing has been seen as the route out of poverty for many a fighter. In Braddock's case, the extremeness of the lows – an inability to make a living during exceptionally dire economic straits – and highs – winning the preeminent boxing title at a time when the sport's popularity was (perhaps) rivaled only by baseball – contribute to the drama. The drama and Braddock's achievements are real enough. However, focusing exclusively on the ups and downs of Braddock's career can result in a distorted picture of his life.

Braddock was a strong but limited fighter who was plagued by chronic hand injuries. After early success as a boxer, he started losing as much as winning. He became a dockworker in New Jersey in order to support his family. Ultimately he was compelled to accept government assistance. Guided by an assertive and faithful manager, Joe Gould, Braddock returned to fighting, and eventually got into contention for the championship. His work as a stevedore with a damaged right hand forced him to start using his left hand more, which ultimately contributed to unexpected success in the ring. In 1935, as he prepared for his title fight with Max Baer, his time on welfare became an issue in a local election, and the idea of a welfare recipient fighting for the heavyweight champion contributed greatly to interest in the fight (and to Braddock's legacy). Using his left, Braddock, a fighter previously known for a powerful right hand and a determined will, won the decision against Baer. The title of an early biography encapsulated the legend: "Relief to Royalty."

These are the outlines of the Braddock story, as retold in Jeremy Schaap's biography of the boxer, *Cinderella Man*. A contemporary newspaper account of Braddock's victory, which Schaap quotes, captures its impact on the public's imagination. "Here was the ideal hero!" wrote Dan Parker of the *New York Daily Mirror*. "An underdog; a modest, likeable fellow; a good family man with a wife and three children; a victim of the depression whose fortune had sunk so low that he had to go on county relief, but whose pride was such that when he got back on his feet, he repaid the county every cent he had received in his lean days; a man whom fortune seemed to have passed by in the ring several years ago, but who realized his dream – all of us cherish – that of getting out of the rut! No wonder almost everyone was pulling for Jimmy to win, though betting the other way."

Although Braddock's months on the dole contributed to his popularity, the fighter never intended for them to be public knowledge. He had been so embarrassed about asking for assistance that he tried to keep it a secret from his parents. But in the spring of 1935, as Braddock was gearing up for his bout with Baer, the mayor of North Bergen, New Jersey, who was up for reelection, began charging that his opponent's associates had mismanaged the relief system. To make his point, he questioned how someone preparing to fight for the heavyweight championship of the world could have needed or deserved government aid. Reporters picked up on the story, and it immediately made Braddock, who legitimately qualified for the aid he received, a sympathetic figure.

According to Schaap, "millions of Americans" rooted for Braddock against Baer "not because Braddock was particularly exciting to watch, but because he personified their own struggles. Like so many of them, he had been humbled by forces beyond his control. Like so many of them, he had been devastated by a system that he assumed was stable. Like so many of them, he had been forced to ask for help." He cites sportswriter Red Smith, who explained, "His time was the Great Depression and he was a man of his time."

Schaap admits that the fighter's rags-to-riches career easily lends itself to underdog clichés and dramatic exaggerations. Near the end of the book, Schaap observes that "Braddock was reduced quickly from a real, indomitable human being to a fairy-tale cliché. The writers could not resist packaging his story in such a fashion...." Schaap cannot completely resist this tendency either. Perhaps the clearest indication of his conforming to the restatement of legend rather than presentation of a full-scale biography is the consignment of Braddock's story after winning the championship to a brief epilogue. Thus, thirty-nine years of his life, more than half of it, are simply perfunctorily tacked on in a few pages at the end of the book. The propensity for clichés also takes the form of a fondness for superlatives, which Schaap demonstrates in his subtitle – "James Braddock, Max Baer, and the Greatest Upset in Boxing History" – and throughout the book. (The betting odds against Buster Douglas beating Mike Tyson were much greater than against Braddock beating Baer, which would suggest that the former was a greater upset.) It's not enough to describe Braddock's training for his fight with Baer as very intense. Instead, his camp is called "the most grueling ever conceived." As the new champion after dethroning Primo Carnera, Baer didn't simply have numerous female fans; rather, "It's quite possible that in the late spring and early summer of 1934, Max Baer received more love letters from more women than any other man ever received." (Who's keeping these records?) Schaap more than once claims that millions of people assumed Baer would remain champion for a decade. He asserts this even as he reports on Baer's often lackadaisical approach to training, which was well known at the time. However, building up Baer as a threat contributes to the Braddock legend.

Although Schaap focuses primarily on Braddock, he also relates Baer's story, and in doing so presents a more complex character than Braddock. Whereas Braddock was a hard worker devoted to his profession, Baer was naturally talented but deeply ambivalent about boxing. He developed an oddly schizophrenic reputation as both a killer and a clown. Frankie Campbell died thirteen hours after Baer severely beat him in a 1930 bout. This occurred during a period of adamant calls for the abolishment of boxing, and Baer was even arrested for manslaughter after the fight. Ernie Schaaf died after fighting Carnera in 1933, but some observers believed the real cause or at least a contributing factor was the damage Baer inflicted in his fight with Schaaf in 1932. Baer was uncomfortable with the very nature and inherent risks of his sport. He expressed a dislike for boxing even as he excelled at it. While he enjoyed the trapping of fame, he was troubled by the possibility of killing opponents. This may caused him to hold back rather than giving his all in subsequent fights. He often fooled around in an effort to amuse spectators with his antics rather than with his boxing ability. Trainers got frustrated with his refusal to prepare seriously for fights. Nevertheless, Baer assembled the better career record, with 72 wins (53 by knockout) and 12 losses. Braddock's less distinguished record was 46 wins (27 by knockout), 23 losses and 4 draws.

Still, according to Schaap, "Baer was no match for Braddock as the darling of the casual fan. No one could relate to him – he was too rich, too good-looking, too strong, too talented. Everyone could relate to Jim Braddock, who was not too rich, too good-looking, too strong, or too talented." If this was in fact the case, it supports Smith's comment about Braddock being of his time. Braddock's Everyman image may have been appealing during the Depression. Nowadays, the qualities attributed to Baer are not a detriment to popularity (think of Oscar De La Hoya), and lacking those characteristics is unlikely to win a fighter fans (think of John Ruiz).

In Schaap's view, "great champions usually are fashioned by adversity." Things came too easily for Baer, he believes, while Braddock constantly confronted difficulties. While there is some truth to this measure of greatness, it is far too simplistic. One major sign of a boxing champion's greatness, after all, is successful defenses of his title. Both Baer and Braddock lost their first title defenses, and neither ever had another shot at the championship. After exposing the shortcoming of the giant Carnera, Baer lost to Braddock one year later. After taking Baer's title, Braddock did not defend it for two years, and then lost it to Joe Louis in 1937. Braddock only fought once more, when he scored a win against Tommy Farr. In contrast, Louis defended his title 25 times. He also compiled a record of 68 wins (with 54 knockouts) and just 3 losses. Louis reigned as undisputed champion until retiring (temporarily) in 1949.

While Braddock might not rate as one of the all-time greats, he does have an undeniably good story. And Schaap supplies the necessary context that helps explain Braddock's popularity during his day. While the particular features and feats an era demands of its heroes may change, the cherished dream of overcoming obstacles endures, and writers continue to seek its embodiment. Like others before him, Schaap finds it in James J. Braddock.

And maybe one of these days we'll rescue a fascinating sport, full of brave warriors and honest practitioners, from the gutter which it still finds so congenial and profitable.

– Budd Schulberg
1995 Foreword to *The Harder They Fall* (1947)

PART II

RED & BLUE CORNERS

HEALTH & SAFETY

In 1998, the International Labor Office (ILO) published the revised fourth edition of its *Encyclopaedia of Occupational Health and Safety*. The ILO is a specialized agency of the United Nations concerned with all matters related to the world of work, and its *Encyclopaedia* aims to provide a comprehensive compendium of ideas as part of an effort to "hasten the day in which occupational death and disease is a rarity in the world."

The third of the four volumes covers "Industries and Occupations," describing all sorts of work and what can be done to make it safer. Volume Three, which exceeds 1,200 pages of small print, examines jobs ranging from airplane building to zoo keeping. The section on entertainment and the arts includes a chapter on professional sports, which devotes a single short paragraph to "Martial Arts and Boxing" – less space than is given to either soccer or baseball.

That the authoritative publication on work and its associated dangers slights an obviously hazardous endeavor is symbolic of a problem in boxing – a lack of reliable information among boxers about what can be done to make the sport safer. Boxers as well as trainers need to be able to make informed decisions about training regimens, nutrition, equipment and all matters that directly affect fighters' health.

The very nature of the sport contributes to the problem of obtaining useful facts about health and safety, since boxing, unfortunately, is in many respects defined by what it lacks. It doesn't have a central governing body along the lines of baseball, football, soccer, basketball and other sports. In the United States, there are numerous state and tribal commissions, in those states that regulate boxing at all. Moreover, boxing is an international sport, with other regulatory bodies in other countries. Unlike most other sports, boxing has no association or union advocating for the athletes' interests. It doesn't have a coherent system of ranking fighters. Instead, there are conflicting ratings issued by a variety of organizations and publications, which results in the sport not even having recognized champions in the various weight divisions. Crucially, there are no uniformly enforced medical guidelines.

In sports like baseball and basketball, the organizational structure affords some protection for athletes. Most athletes in these sports emerge from school programs run by coaches and administrators who are accountable to the institutions that employ them. Few schools have boxing programs, and boxers are left to themselves to find trainers and managers. Most athletes who turn pro play for leagues with clear rules run by individuals with defined responsibilities. In contrast, boxers work in a fairly chaotic, largely ad hoc series of arrangements put together by representatives whose roles may entail serious conflicts of interests. And for many fighters, boxing is a second job. The various athletic commissions that regulate local boxing events may be adequately funded and staffed by knowledgeable and conscientious individuals. Then again, they may not.

Further complicating matters is that boxing operates through a sort of apprentice system in which knowledge is past along from trainers, frequently former fighters themselves, to the younger generation. Whether trainers' insight into the fundamentals of the sports is complemented by awareness about what is best for their fighters' wellbeing is an open question. All too often, fights continue long after it is clear that one fighter is being punished and has no realistic hope of victory. The ringside physicians might not have an obvious reason – such as a severe and bloody cut over an eye – to stop the fight. There might not be a single point – like the fighter becoming trapped and unable to defend himself from a flurry of blows – where the referee could intervene. Instead, the fighter might hold his hands up and move forward – into repeated, thumping, cumulative blows to the head that don't knock him down but undoubtedly do damage. In these situations, the failure of the boxer's corner to end the fight makes the question of their concern for their fighter's health a pressing one. Furthermore, some trainers regard ringside physicians' brief examinations of struggling fighters between rounds not as basic precautions but as intrusions.

Given these circumstances, the shortage of applicable health and safety information is no surprise. This is not to say that such information does not exist. There have been scientific studies of the effects of boxing on fighters; there are methods of maintaining or losing weight that are generally regarded as safe; there's recognition of the need for rest in order to recuperate.

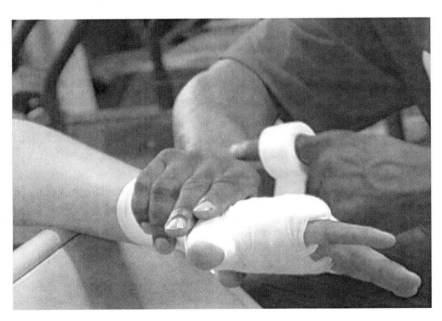

But the existence of such information is one thing, access to it another.

The example of the ILO encyclopedia remains telling – and troubling – in this regard. The small assessment it offers on boxing is debatable, at best. It suggests that headgear "help[s] soften the impact of a blow." The article notes that boxers are at risk for "long-term brain damage," but the implication that headgear offers protection is hardly a resolved matter, since many in the sport believe headgear does little beyond avoiding cuts on fighters' faces. Beyond that, headgear and gloves probably do more to protect the hands of those doing the hitting than the heads of those being hit. (The sentence in the encyclopedia on potential hand injuries likens them to those suffered by volleyball players.)

There are efforts to collect and share various types of data among regulators; this is the reason for being for the Association of Boxing Commissions, for instance. There is no equivalent for fighters and trainers when it comes to health and safety information. Supporters of a U.S. federal boxing commission have suggested that a licensing mechanism for trainers and gyms would help protect fighters by ensuring that trainers are qualified and gym owners abide by rules regarding suspensions. Whatever its merits might be, such a system is unlikely to be established any time soon. Boxers may begin fighting at a young age, when they necessarily rely on others to take care of them, and they may need to develop a sense of invulnerability in order to thrive in the sport. But they ultimately must take responsibility for themselves, and in order to do this they need accurate information about their sport and its hazards. The *Ringside and Training Principles* handbook issued under the auspices of the Nevada State Athletic Commission (and the related website) are steps in this direction. However, unless he or she fights in Nevada or somehow knows to request a copy or visit the site, a boxer might not know about these resources. And, given boxing's global status, language is another factor. (The ILO encyclopedia has been translated into several languages.)

There is no shortage of data on most aspects of boxing. There are dozens of websites dedicated to covering fights and reporting on upcoming events. There are several magazines offering glossy photos of the elite fighters' bouts. It's easy to look up records. (Even the ILO gets some things right: "Agility, speed and strength minimize the combatant's injuries.") But there are relatively few ways for the fighters to educate themselves about their own protection, including about the need to select cornermen who not only will try to help them win but also try to preserve their lives.

It could be helpful if more of the boxing websites and magazines regularly addressed these issues in accessible language. "Train the trainer" sessions organized by athletic commissions or other groups and run by ringside physicians could also be beneficial. There have been moves made over the years, such as shortening championships fights, moving weigh-ins to the day before, adding a fourth rope to the ring and requiring certain medical tests, that have made boxing safer. Helping fighters to look out for themselves would be another positive step.

THERE ARE NO EASY ANSWERS

It would be safe to bet that everyone with an interest in boxing – from fighter to fan – has at some point endured a discussion with someone who dislikes the sport and dismisses it as people beating each other in a barbaric display of the worst of mankind's nature for the sick pleasure of ghoulish observers. Some members of the media have felt that way. For example, *Civilta Cattolica*, a magazine affiliated with the Vatican, gave voice to this negative view of the sport when it likened boxing to a "legalized form of attempted murder."

But those in the boxing community know that the sport is not mere brawling. It's more complicated than that. Yes, boxing entails people hitting each other, but there's also technique; there's savvy. Boxing involves skills honed through training, and its practitioners are athletes, not brutes. The critics overlook the complexity of boxing while the would-be reformers of the sport run the risk of oversimplifying matters.

Tragedies like the death of Leavander Johnson may – actually should – prompt those in the boxing world to pause and reflect on the violence inherent in the sport and its very real consequences. On September 17, 2005, Johnson collapsed soon after losing his International Boxing Federation lightweight title defense against Jesus Chavez in Las Vegas. Despite immediate medical attention, including brain surgery, Johnson died a few days later.

Efforts to avoid future severe injuries and fatalities, no matter how well intentioned, must start with an understanding that making boxing safer is no simple matter.

In an article on Johnson's death in the September 29 edition of the *Wall Street Journal*, Gordon Marino (a philosophy professor) concludes, "It would be reasonable for professional boxers to follow the amateurs and don headgear and more thickly padded gloves. But that has been tried and fight fans will not buy it. That is why some of Leavander Johnson's blood is on all of our ticket stubs."

The real question is not whether using headgear and heavier gloves is "reasonable" but whether it would help to protect fighters. It might appear as though the answer is obvious, but it is not.

A few years ago, I interviewed Dr. Flip Homansky, a former member of the Nevada State Athletic Commission (NSAC) and a former ringside physician, as well as Dr. Margaret Goodman, who was ringside at the Johnson-Chavez fight. Both expressed some doubt about headgear's ability to lessen a fighter's risk of brain injury. As Homansky pointed out, there are several factors to take into consideration, not the least of which is that headgear adds weight to the head, which can result in it moving more from a blow. And the brain bouncing around inside the skull is what can lead to damage. Homansky also said headgear can, in certain situations, limit a fighter's vision, which can have obvious effects. For one, it can cause boxers to hold their heads up in order to see when they should be tucking their chins to protect themselves. Homansky also pointed out that there are psychological aspects. Some fighters would believe headgear provide the ultimate protection. As a result, they may not take appropriate defensive measures. Headgear helps fighters avoid being cut, he acknowledged, but it might not do a great deal to protect them from brain damage.

Even if headgear and heavier gloves did reduce the number of knockouts, they could increase the number of blows a boxer must endure. If those blows weren't strong enough to twist the brain on its stem and cause a knockout, they could still result in injuries from a greater number of accumulated punches.

When I spoke to them in Las Vegas, Homansky and Goodman said their major concern is what happens in gyms, where fighters may injure themselves, or start sparring too soon after a fight (regardless of whether they won or lost or whether they were knocked out), or get knocked out while in training but continue to spar or proceed with a scheduled fight. Fighters spend far more time in the gym than they do in actual professional fights, and what occurs there can have lasting effects and can contribute to injuries and deaths.

After the Johnson-Chavez fight, Goodman – in a widely circulated observation that Marino partially repeats – said: "Something is wrong. I don't know what it is and I don't know what needs to be changed, but we need to re-evaluate the entire way we approach the testing and treatment of boxers. These kids trust their lives to us and we are failing them. The commission is going to sit down and look at everything again and again and again."

Goodman, the current chairman of the NSAC Medical Advisory Board, knows boxing and as anyone who has ever spoken to her about the sport and her job can attest, she cares sincerely and deeply about boxers. She is also smart enough to know that avoiding another boxing fatality is not an easy thing to achieve. There's no immediate apparent cure-all that was overlooked or ignored.

Soon after Goodman acknowledged that she didn't have all the answers, the NSAC established the Advisory Committee on Boxer Health and Safety to try and find some. The committee consists of former commissioners Sig Rogich, Dr. Luther Mack and Dr. James Nave; former NSAC Medical Advisory Board member Dr. Charles Ruggeroli; and Harvey J. Munford of the Nevada Legislature.

No doubt the committee will seek to find real solutions, not easy (and inadequate) answers. Homansky and Goodman are, I believe, willing to look at things, including the potential value of headgear "again and again and again," and I hope the new committee will come up with ways to help.

While Marino's figurative remark about collective responsibility may have some merit, we owe it to Johnson and all fighters to be serious about these matters. That means trying to respond in a meaningful way, not assuming that there's a quick fix.

Postscript: While the premise of this piece – that there are no simple ways to make boxing safer – is valid, the conclusion that a special committee appointed by those already responsible for oversight would achieve improvement, or try to, strikes me in retrospect as unduly sanguine. Not long after the fight described here, Goodman resigned as a Nevada ringside physician, citing infighting over reform among the state commission and doctors. She subsequently stepped down from the NSAC Medical Advisory Board as well.

A First-Class Sport

Boxing is good for you. That idea might sound strange to twenty-first century ears on either side of eyes not accustomed to seeing a bright side to violence. Yet it has a long history and continues to have committed adherents, and not only among those whose livelihoods depend on the sport. A long tradition of belief in the benefits of boxing persists among police officers, for instance, and police athletic leagues factor significantly in boxing history. Police departments do not encourage boxing because of an unstated institutional aim of helping in the creation of future champions, though this has been the outcome more than once. Instead, they do so for another out-of-fashion notion: that boxing is good not only for individuals but for communities.

Theodore Roosevelt regarded boxing, "whether professional or amateur, as a first-class sport." In his 1913 memoir, he says that as New York City's police commissioner in the late nineteenth century he discovered "that the establishment of a boxing club in a tough neighborhood always tended to do away with knifing and gun-fighting among the young fellows who would otherwise have been in murderous gangs." The key was to give potential law-breakers something positive to do. "Many of these young fellows were not naturally criminals at all, but they had to have some outlet for their activities." Even though later, when serving as governor, he signed a bill outlawing professional boxing, he did this because "the prize ring had become hopelessly debased and demoralized." He objected to the "brutalizing" business of boxing, not to boxing itself. "I shall always maintain that boxing contests themselves make good, healthy sport," he says in *An Autobiography*. The advocate of the strenuous life boxed with prizefighter friends as governor and later when he was president.

John McCain, a great admirer of Roosevelt, also sees boxing as a first-class sport but worries about the corrupt business practices surrounding it. McCain devotes a chapter in *Worth the Fighting For* to praising Roosevelt, both for his efforts to develop the branch of the military in which he served before entering politics and for his character and industry generally. "For the McCains of the United States Navy ... presidents just didn't get much better than Teddy Roosevelt." More ebulliently, he exclaims: "my God, what a superior man TR was." TR said the sole objection he had to boxing was "the crookedness that has attended its commercial development," and McCain would certainly agree. When I interviewed him in the summer of 2002 about the sport, McCain expressed concern about the "exploitation of boxers" as a result of the "predatory practices" of "greedy promoters." He discussed "abuses" in the conduct of the business of boxing and predicted that there would be "more scandals" in an activity that has become synonymous with scandal. When talking about boxing itself, however, he saw plenty to praise as well as criticize. "It's given us some of the highest and most exhilarating moments in sports and it's given us some of the most disgraceful." He referred to the "uplifting things about boxing" such as the "magnificent display of courage" boxers like Mickey Ward and Arturo Gatti offered when they fought.

More than a century after Roosevelt led New York's police department, another of the city's police commissioners also briefly held the position of chairman of the state's athletic commission. Ray Kelly brought the policeman's longstanding faith in boxing to actual regulation of what he called the "much troubled sport." Like both Roosevelt and McCain, he sees "abuses" plaguing the sport but finds plenty to admire about fighters. "The best thing about boxing is the boxers themselves," he told me during the period when he had the dual roles. He respects their hard work, determination, and willingness to participate in "the most demanding sport situation you can imagine."

Another Teddy – trainer and boxing commentator Teddy Atlas – was precisely the sort of "young fellow" that concerned Roosevelt, and boxing played a determinative role in turning him away from self-destructive criminal behavior. When Atlas was a teenager facing gun and robbery charges, trainer Cus D'Amato testified on his behalf and Atlas received probation on the condition that he remain living with D'Amato, who soon after Atlas's day in court would start training a juvenile delinquent named Mike Tyson, who was released from reform school into D'Amato's custody. Even before becoming involved with D'Amato, Atlas had experience with the sort of club Roosevelt endorses. "In those days the cops tried to get problem kids involved in boxing in the Police Athletic League," Atlas writes of his youth in 1970s Staten Island in *Atlas: From the Streets to the Ring: A Son's Struggle to Become a Man*. He says PAL boxing "was a good program in lots of ways. It helped kids." Atlas suggests that his long career in the sport, including his guiding Michael Moorer to the heavyweight championship, can be traced back to his time "boxing in an old laundry room in a rough project." Even though young Atlas continued to steal and get into street fights even after he started boxing and then, because back problems forced him to stop competing, training fighters, he eventually went straight. Atlas says he would love to see the charitable foundation he started one day open homes for troubled and abused kids where living would be "centered around a boxing program," which could help give them "care, direction, instruction, discipline, accountability, and dreams."

This desire to aid children's development through boxing is common among both trainers and cops. In his memoir, *Serenity,* Ralph Wiley recalls his early days as a sportswriter on the boxing beat and visits he paid to the New Oakland Boxing Club, where he met a police officer representing the PAL who worked with young fighters. "Boxing breeds respect," Jerry Blueford told Wiley. "For the other man. I don't care if any of these kids ever become pros, or even good amateurs for that matter. I'm trying to get them into something they can work at. Off the streets. If they leave here in a couple of years and rob a bank, at least they didn't rob it while they were here." In a section that harkens back to Roosevelt's remark about tough neighborhoods, Wiley describes visiting Detroit's Kronk Boxing Club, in "the bottom of the rundown bunker of a recreation center on an otherwise barren lot of the decayed inner city." Wiley calls the place "a haven of sorts for the children of Detroit" where he cannot help being impressed by its principal, trainer-manager Emanuel Steward, because of "how Emanuel had overcome long odds, and helped his young men overcome long odds, just to be strong and functional."

Although the police may be more concerned with giving kids something lawful to do and connecting them with mentors who can help them become functional than with moving them toward athletic success, individual policemen and particular PALs have helped form a number of champions, including Muhammad Ali. According to McCain, one of the best things about boxing is the "opportunity that it gives for someone who might otherwise never have a chance to achieve fame and fortune." Discovering his bicycle had been stolen, Cassius Clay, as the twelve-year-old was then known, wanted to report his loss to the police. Directed to a gymnasium underneath Louisville's

Columbia Auditorium where officer Joe Martin trained youngsters how to box, the future fighter met his first trainer. Martin's new trainee impressed him with displays of an intense drive: "he had more determination than most boys.... He was a kid willing to make the sacrifices necessary to achieve something worthwhile in sports." Ali, according to Thomas Hauser's biography of the boxer, believes the endeavor for which he willingly made sacrifices, helped him lead a clean, healthy life: "I trained six days a week, and never drank or smoked a cigarette.... Boxing kept me out of trouble."

Larry Holmes, who succeeded Ali as heavyweight champion, first boxed as a ten-year-old in PAL-organized bouts in Pennsylvania. "The PAL would gather us kids to put on backroom matches for the various civic clubs ... like the Kiwanis and Rotary Clubs, and the VFW. All these organizations, not to mention the firefighters, had social clubs, and on Wednesday nights you would see us peewees whacking away at each other with oversize boxing gloves," Holmes recalls in his autobiography. When, years later, he became serious about the sport, he started training at a PAL gym. Prior to committing himself to boxing, he had been a petty criminal, stealing car radios and selling marijuana. He also took drugs, though an unpleasant, hallucinatory experience with hashish prompted him to forswear drugs forever. "Everyone in boxing knew ... that when you fight Larry Holmes you're going up against a fighter whose body and mind are not messed up with drugs," he says, referring to himself in the third person. He found himself through fighting: "People express themselves differently. Painters paint, writers write, dancers dance. I discovered I needed physical contact to let what was in me come out."

Youngsters looking for ways to express themselves, or to vent what Roosevelt calls their "animal spirits," are not likely to have the opportunity to do so by boxing at school. George

Plimpton begins *Shadow Box,* his first-person account of a writer confronting a professional boxer in the ring (in order to write about it) and other musings about the sport, by recalling his school's mandatory boxing matches, which he hated:

> At school, once a month, we were required to box down in the gym – paired off, with enormous gloves tied to our pipestem arms. When the master blew his whistle, we strained and lifted up these monstrous pillows to push and flail them at each other. It was the worst time of the month.

Of course, a child's dislike for something does not mean it isn't good for him, but that may be a moot point, since Plimpton's schoolhouse boxing experience had already became rare by the time *Shadow Box* first appeared in 1977.

College professor Carlo Rotella believes people can learn much from boxing that has relevance beyond the ring. In *Cut Time,* he says boxing teaches subjects that might not immediately appear to be connected with the sport, including lessons "about the virtues and limits of craft, about the need to impart meaning to hard facts by enfolding them in stories and spectacle, about getting old, about distance and intimacy, and especially about education itself: boxing conducts an endless workshop in the teaching and learning of knowledge with consequences." Less abstractly, Rotella says boxing can foster the development of practical habits such as "sharpening and strengthening yourself through disciplined application, [and] learning to protect yourself by doing things regularly and the right way."

Although boxing has disappeared from most U.S. college athletic departments, its return to campuses could have some benefits. In *A Beautiful Sickness,* Hauser advocates the formation of a college boxing league, partially because it could improve the diminished image of the sport, but also because of what it could do for young athletes. "College boxing would be good for the fighters," he asserts. "It would give them additional options in life and help improve their lives." To illustrate his argument, he mentions boxers who could not afford college and joined the military (where boxing traditions persist) or dropped out of school in order to pursue professional boxing dreams. "It's good to get in the ring and get hit and hit somebody," McCain said to me when reflecting on the boxing done at the Naval Academy, and it is not hard to imagine his hero TR having said the same thing. ("Of course boxing should be encouraged in the army and navy," Roosevelt writes.) However, the National Collegiate Athletic Association disagreed with such an assessment. It discontinued boxing soon after the post-fight death of a college boxer in 1960. (Indeed, boxing is not *always* good for you. Then again, neither are some of the conventional collegiate sports, such as football, which can also cause injury and death.)

With boxing moving from the mainstream to the margins of the sporting world, boxing gyms, in order to survive, have had to expand their membership beyond professional fighters. Writing in the late 1990s, Holmes describes how Gleason's Gym changed from the spare, smelly space it had been when he first visited one of its earlier locations in 1970. The Brooklyn incarnation "adapted to this era of boxing chic, counting among its members numerous stockbrokers and women who do white-collar workouts, at the same time that your regular fighters train."

Nevertheless, boxing gyms continue to operate in the ways Roosevelt envisioned. Gleason's, for one, perpetuates the policemen's view of boxing's benefits though its Give a Kid a Dream program. Frequently, teachers or parents or cops will refer kids having problems at school or starting to get into serious trouble to Gleason's, and proprietor Bruce Silverglade will arrange for the youngsters to work with trainers. "The man with the less to lose outside the ring usually has the most to gain inside it," Wiley observed, and the kids directed to

Gleason's come from households which would not be able to pay the membership fees Silverglade agrees to waive. They do not attend the sort of schools Plimpton did. Though in some instances a child might need the sustained exertion of rigorous training mainly for the sake of physical fitness, many others end up boxing for the reasons identified by New York police commissioners: to learn to apply themselves, to practice self-discipline and to develop a vigorous work ethic. Often, trainers become father figures for the fighters, who frequently do come from single-family homes. I heard a kid at Gleason's say his trainer not only taught him how to fight but also taught him how to be a man. Teddy and Teddy would approve.

So would Katherine Dunn, though she goes on to point out that women as well as men can benefit from time spent in boxing gyms. Like Roosevelt and Atlas, she praises the sport's contribution to individuals' reflexes, stamina and strength. In *One Ring Circus,* she similarly observes that "the most urgent reason" for training is "to get kids off the street before they get tangled up in drugs or gangs or other forms of destruction," and offers an anecdote to support the thesis. She recalls hearing a nine-year-old newcomer to a boxing gym express his goal for adulthood: "I'm gonna get me a string of bitches and be a flash pimp." She learns that while he did later spend some time in juvenile detention, he subsequently returned to boxing, became a Golden Gloves champ and then went onto college and a teaching job. Dunn sees the aggressiveness of boxing as a positive good, linked as it is to the survival instinct. The sport perpetuates and hones a quality human beings – male and female – do not want to lose. For this reason, she regards Dallas Malloy as a hero. As a teenager, Malloy sued U.S. Amateur Boxing for gender discrimination and won, forcing the organization to permit girls to compete and, more generally, making boxing more widely available to anyone who might need what it can provide.

Larry Holmes says that if he had not quit doing drugs and dedicated himself to boxing, rather than becoming heavyweight champion, he might have ended up like one of his former friends who continued along the path he chose not to keep following: shot to death by law enforcement agents. PAL organizers and supporters around the country no doubt take a small measure of pride that he and many others instead opted to pursue the opportunities offered by a first-class sport. Boxing, they just might say, is good for you.

"What do you think about? I mean, specifically what kind of thing?"

"Well, I'm thinking of what the other guy is doing, that I can use. You know? I mean, Doc has always studied the guys I fight and we've pretty much worked it out, but you actually have to fight the guy to find out."

"They all have patterns," Doc said. "I don't care who they are."

"Then fighters are like writers," Dave said.

"The good ones have more patterns than the others," Doc said. "That's all."

W.C. Heinz, *The Professional* (1958)

PART III

WRITERS & FIGHTERS

ROLLINS ON THE ROAD

From late July to early September 2006, the Rollins Band toured the United States with punk-rockers-with-staying-power X. The version of Henry Rollins's band with Sim Cain on drums, Melvin Gibbs on bass, Chris Haskett on guitar and Theo Van Rock on sound, which recorded the albums *Weight* and *Come in and Burn*, had last performed together in 1997. Vocalist Rollins kept a journal of his preparation for and experiences during the As the World Burns Tour. His own publishing house issued his account a mere two months after his band played the final scheduled show. Precisely what makes the life examined in *A Dull Roar: What I Did on My Summer Deracination 2006* potentially interesting to mere mortals – Rollins's prodigious work rate and superhuman ability to achieve – can lessen the quality of his writing. Yet he offers an at-times compelling portrait of a highly motivated performer at middle age.

The quickness of *A Dull Roar*'s appearance is all the more impressive given the other activities Rollins juggled (and described). In addition to band practice and concerts, there was acting in a horror movie filmed in Vancouver, taping segments in Los Angeles for his Independent Film Channel program and negotiating terms for another season, giving spoken word performances in England and elsewhere, working on a weekly radio show, planning a USO tour and – endlessly – writing. He reveals his dedication to rapid publication by writing in the book itself about the process of proofreading and correcting the first part of the manuscript well before the series of events he set out to record – the rock shows – had even been completed.

His productivity and commitment to his work is mightily impressive, but the very same drive to get a lot of work done undermines his efforts as a chronicler of his busy life. Rollins acknowledges that he has "always struggled with writing." *A Dull Roar* and his other books suggest that precisely what makes his relentless drive to achieve worth recording is also part of what keeps him from becoming a better writer. At the end of each day, he records what he did, and he frequently looks ahead to what's next. He doesn't spend much time looking back. He's fully aware of this inclination. "As soon as the tour is over, I have to get onto the next thing, whatever it will be, as soon as I can," he writes when there are just a few shows left to play. "I think it is best when completing a tour, to treat it like a magazine with no more bullets and eject it from the weapon and reload with the next thing and not look back." He's eager to put in time – all of his time – working on multiple projects, but that means limiting the time devoted to any one of them.

His documentation of his movement from project to project reads more like solid raw material for a memoir than a completed, polished work. Rollins does not know at the beginning of the book how the story is going to end. He relays his experiences as they occur. This does give the telling some immediacy. However, the journal form, with daily entries ranging from few lines to a few pages, includes inherent limitations. He mentions possible future projects, such as another season of *The Henry Rollins Show* on IFC and another USO tour (having already visited troops in Afghanistan, Iraq, Kuwait, Qatar and elsewhere), but these matters are not resolved within the period covered. (After the book appeared, he did begin work on new episodes of his TV show, and in December 2006 the United Service Organization announced Rollins's seventh USO/Armed Forces Entertainment tour to visit troops in the Persian Gulf region.) He also repeats himself, stating particular personal preferences – such as for

Ali-Foreman, 1974

being alone or for living in hotel rooms rather than at his house in L.A. – multiple times.

He plans for victory while knowing failure is a practical certainty. For Rollins, performing live music is analogous to going into battle. His style is confrontational. Referring to the 1974 "Rumble in the Jungle," he likens himself to a boxer: "The show is George Foreman. I am Ali. I am going to take a beating but I will prevail. That's how this music is. It is a fight." Given the very physical nature of a Rollins performance, a great deal of his preparation for the tour involved an intensive training regimen. Though in his mid-40s during this period, Rollins maintained a fighter's physique and threw himself entirely into his intense and sweaty shows. However, his band mates do not share his view of music as conflict or his disciplined approach to exercise. He questions the others' dedication and suspects that the end of the tour will be the end of the Rollins Band, at least the incarnation of it that went on the road with X. "All the training and preparation I did is just being laughed at so there's no point in thinking about any further work with this line up," he writes on August 23, 2006. "There's no way I'm going to feel like this any longer than I have to."

Since *A Dull Roar* ends with the tour it describes, there's no way for the reader to know if the way he felt then is the way he still felt after he had some time to look back on what happened. After all, while some of what he does (like acting) he does just to keep busy and put some money in the bank, music is not just another job for him. "It's all that matters," he announces at the end.

Because of his disappointment with the tour and his inability to see a future with the band that bears his name, *A Dull Roar* reads like a log of disappointment. Yet because he expects defeat he prepares for it and even thrives on its imminence. "Failure is a motivator," he writes early in the journal. "Knowing I am going to fail anyway at least gives me a sense of humor about it all and allows resolve to take the lead in front of ambition. Going down swinging is what I reckon the last half of my life is about." Rollins expresses great admiration for Albert Camus, and it's really no surprise, since both writers prize perseverance. And there's a remarkable steadfastness in his commitment to soldiering on in his work despite knowing things won't work out that makes *A Dull Roar* inspiring and its flawed structure strangely appropriate to its message.

GOING OFF COURSE

WITH MELVILLE & LIEBLING

Herman Melville had a propensity for what A.J. Liebling calls "labyrinthine digressions," a tendency Liebling shares. Too many readers, I believe, mistake Melville's elaborate discursiveness for a weakness, but the digressions are not beside the point – they are the point. I witnessed failures to follow Melville in a group of friends who met regularly, for a time, to talk about books. Before discussing *Moby-Dick*, the book club showed signs of inevitable dissolution. Though Melville did not wreck the book club, he certainly helped to sink it.

When possible, the group met at places relevant to the month's reading. To talk about a novel set partially on Coney Island, for instance, we converged at a bar on the boardwalk in the shadow of the Wonder Wheel. When *Pride and Prejudice* was the assignment, we met at a restaurant specializing in English food. I don't think of Jane Austen as a fish and chips fan, which I took as working in the venue's favor. I cannot read her books without hoping her insipid characters' villages burn down and their horses run away. These outings introduced a social element that did not always lend itself to serious discussion, and members' ideas of what was worth reading diverged significantly anyway. In retrospect I'm surprised a majority ever voted to select *Moby-Dick,* which we discussed in Battery Park, near the part of Manhattan where the novel opens. Returning to the novel after at least a decade since last reading it, I enjoyed the winding journey of the *Pequod* more than I had remembered. Few shared my enthusiasm. One pulled out a condensed version of Melville's irreducible novel, igniting envy in some others who thought *Moby-Dick* needed a severe editor to keep its narrator focused. I knew our group would not last much longer, at least not with me as a member.

I would agree that Melville's expansive style proved less successful on some of his earlier excursions. *Mardi* can be trying, and *Redburn* does read like just one damn thing after another. But with *Moby-Dick* – with its quests not just for a certain whale but also for knowledge itself – he found the problem to match the writerly solution he devised.

The many chapters that strike some readers as extraneous – the ones cut from that indefensible shortened edition – are what make *Moby-Dick* more than a simple seafaring yarn. Certainly it can be read as an adventure story of a crew led by an intensely driven, perhaps crazed, captain in pursuit of the white whale that had ripped off his leg. But all the chapters that don't directly advance that story are what make the novel so much more: a skeptic's consideration of belief in god, a look at race and slavery in the United States, a chronicle of industrialization and man's attempt to conquer and harness nature, a depiction of burgeoning American imperial activities and, ultimately, a portrait of men hunting for spermaceti and revenge but also meaning. The confrontation and contest with the limits of human knowledge hold the story together like a sturdy chain. Removing those parts – those digressions – ruins the thing.

Bored readers in my now long-defunct book club have an ally of sorts in Nathaniel Hawthorne. In a journal entry from 1856, Hawthorne describes his last meeting with Melville, which occurred in Liverpool, where Hawthorne was serving as American Consul. Although Hawthorne does not specifically discuss *Moby-Dick*, he describes his former neighbor's restless mind and unsatisfied search for meaning in a manner that relates directly to what Melville does in his best-known novel (and merits quoting at length).

> Herman Melville came to see me at the Consulate, looking much as he used to do (a little paler, and perhaps a little sadder), in a rough outside coat, and with his characteristic gravity and reserve of manner.... Melville has not been well, of late; ... and no doubt has suffered from too constant literary occupation, pursued without much success, latterly; and his writings, for a long while past, have indicated a morbid state of mind.... Melville, as he always does, began to reason of Providence and futurity, and of everything that lies beyond human ken, and informed me that he had "pretty much made up his mind to be annihilated"; but still he does not seem to rest in that anticipation; and, I think, will never rest until he gets hold of a definite belief. It is strange how he persists – and has persisted ever since I knew him, and probably long before – in wandering to-and-fro over these deserts, as dismal and monotonous as the sand hills amid which we were sitting. He can neither believe, nor be comfortable in his unbelief; and he is too honest and courageous not to try to do one or the other. If he were a religious man, he would be one of the most truly religious and reverential; he has a very high and noble nature, and better worth immortality than most of us.

Melville's ceaseless philosophizing evidently wearies Hawthorne. While he expressed admiration for *Moby-Dick*, which Melville dedicated to him, Hawthorne would probably sympathize with readers who tire of the many chapters that don't propel its story straightly forward. I imagine the author of *The Scarlet Letter* feeling relief when his voluble old friend finally left his office.

Unwilling readers also receive backing from a less, well, diplomatic critic. Clive James says he enjoys "narrative flow." Attempting to endure *Moby-Dick*, he found "Melville's ocean clung like tar." In his own wildly digressive book, *Cultural Amnesia*, James, in a piece nominally about Jorge Luis Borges, says "there is surely a case for saying that the story of Captain Ahab's contest with the white whale is one of those books you can't get started with even after you've finished reading them." If *Moby-Dick* bears traces of the morbidity Hawthorne finds in its author, it is also enlivened by an unbound exuberance which James overlooks. There's gloom *and* there's humor. Melville makes any and every aspect of whaling an opportunity for "wandering to-and-fro," for pursuing the elusive loose-fish of truth.

Ishmael and Ahab share Melville's questing tendencies but direct them to radically different purposes. As narrator, Ishmael gets lost in his reveries as he ponders philosophy, nature, art and whale taxonomy. Ahab, the man of action, is motivated by revenge; his search has a definite object. Both characters use "diving" as a metaphor for their quests for answers. "Beneath this wondrous world upon the surface" there is "another and still stranger world"; satisfaction with surface appearance means embracing ignorance. "Of all divers, thou has dived the deepest," Ahab says to a sperm whale, as though the creature might possesses the answer to his nagging question. Ishmael uses "diving" as a metaphor for learning when expostulating on whaling's eventful tradition, one of the innumerable subjects he plunges into.

The idea of diving for truth leads Ishmael to associate land with the known and water with the unknown, which makes going to sea an education. He finds parallels between the outer world and mental processes:

> Glimpses do ye seem to see of that mortally intolerable truth; that all deep, earnest thinking is but the intrepid effort of the soul to keep the open independence of her sea; while the wildest winds of heaven and earth conspire to cast her on the treacherous, slavish shore?
>
> But in landlessness alone reside the highest truth, shoreless, indefinite as God – so, better is it to perish in that howling infinite, than to be ingloriously dashed upon the lee, even if that were safety.

Pursuing knowledge requires confronting the unknown and perhaps unknowable, which can involve both physical and mental dangers.

> [C]onsider them both, the sea and the land; and do you not find a strange analogy to something in yourself? For as this appalling ocean surrounds the verdant land, so in the soul of man there lies one insular Tahiti, full of peace and joy, but encompassed by the half known life. God keep thee! Push not off from that isle, thou canst never return!

Although their individual responses to life's risks may differ, humans risk sharing the plight of Pip, who when he jumped from a boat was left treading water as "another lonely castaway" until, by chance, he was rescued by the *Pequod*. Confronted with the "intense concentration of self in the middle of such a heartless immensity," Pip goes mad.

In addition to the metaphysical musings that exhaust James and other reluctant readers, Ishmael conveys concrete, earthy ideas. Material concerns counterbalance abstract thought. Indeed, Ishmael connects philosophy and indigestion. "So soon as I hear that such or such a man gives himself out for a philosopher, I conclude that, like the dyspeptic old woman, he must have 'broken his digester.'" He regards religion along the same lines: "Hell is an idea first born on an undigested apple-dumpling...." Ishmael may remain unsure about the meaning of life, but he does have some definite convictions, such as this bit of advice: "if you can get nothing better out of the world, get a good meal out of it, at least." (James, who throughout *Cultural Amnesia* admires aphorisms, misses Melville's talent for them.)

Ishmael, who gets so caught up in his thoughts that he forgets his duties as a crewmember, sometimes expresses skepticism about the relevance of philosophy and religion to daily life. "Methinks we have hugely mistaken this matter of Life and Death. Methinks that what they call my shadow here on earth is my true substance." He remarks on Christian hypocrisy: "Better to sleep with a sober cannibal than a drunken Christian"; "Christian kindness has proved but hollow courtesy." He observes that "a man's religion is one thing, and this practical world another." The same note is struck by the narrator in *White Jacket*, the book Melville wrote immediately before *Moby-Dick:* "For after all, philosophy – that is, the best wisdom that has ever in any way been revealed to our man-of-war world – is but a slough and a mire, with a few tufts of good footing here and there." In later work, Melville focuses intently on the day-to-day uses of philosophy, rather than capital-t Truth. *The Confidence-Man* sees characters questioning what information can be trusted and how it can be exploited, precisely the issues that concern Ahab.

Whatever Ishmael's misgivings about philosophy, he never abandons it. He likens whale heads hanging on either side the *Pequod* to Kant and Locke, only to then suggest that philosophy is useless: "Oh, ye foolish! throw these thunderheads overboard, and then you will float light and right." However, a few pages later, the love of wisdom regains importance for Ishmael, who again finds philosophical aspects in whale heads: "This Right Whale I take to have been a Stoic; the Sperm Whale, a Platonian, who might have taken up Spinoza in his latter years." Alas, not everyone sees the humor in such asides.

The chapter in which Ishmael explores the reasons why "it was the whiteness of the whale that above all things appalled" him does not directly advance the story of the *Pequod's* final whaling expedition, which only Ishmael survives. However, the brilliant digression about the struggle for understanding is vital to *Moby-Dick*. Of the whiteness, Ishmael wonders:

> Is it that by its indefiniteness it shadows forth the heartless voids and immensities of the universe, and thus stabs us from behind with the thought of

annihilation, when beholding the white depths of the milky way? Or is it, that as in essence whiteness is not so much a color as the visible absence of color, and at the same time the concrete of all colors; is it for these reasons that there is such a dumb blankness, full of meaning, in a wide landscape of snows – a colorless, all-color of atheism from which we shrink?

The whiteness of the whale serves as a screen onto which various narratives and interpretations are projected. Yet a screen can also conceal; behind it there may be nothing but the void that unhinged Pip. As Hawthorne said of Melville, Ishmael is troubled by the meaninglessness of the universe as he perceives it, but is also unwilling to stop studying it. He does not stop speculating, or reconsidering. He continues to dive. He does so knowing he will never catch any ultimate meaning.

While both Ishmael and Ahab dive in pursuit of answers, they differ in their attitudes towards the knowable and unknowable. In chapter 89, "Fast-Fish and Loose-Fish," seizing property is described in a manner that resembles Marx's discussion of the primitive accumulation of capital. Slaves, mansions, the salary of a wealthy preacher and colonies are fast-fish – property snatched by the powerful. India was a loose-fish made fast by England, and the United States would make a fast-fish of Mexico. When Ahab reveals his intentions to harpoon one particular whale, Starbuck responds by stressing that the voyage is a business venture, one literally about capturing prey for profit: "I came here to hunt whales, not my commander's vengeance. How many barrels will thy vengeance yield thee even if thou gettest it, Captain Ahab? It will not fetch thee much in our Nantucket market." Business matters arise when Pip jumps from Stubb's whaling boat. By leaving Pip floundering in the water, "Stubb indirectly hinted, that though man loves his fellow, yet man is a money-making animal, which propensity too often interferes with his benevolence." Ishmael's distinction between fast and loose fish, which does not move Ahab any closer to the white whale, stresses the very real consequences of the pursuit of knowledge.

The narrator suggests that meaning is a loose-fish. Presuming, like Ahab does, that it can be made fast will produce tragic results. Though the captain will not abandon his search for Moby Dick, Ishmael accepts that some fish simply cannot be made fast, that some questions cannot be answered. Ishmael's digressive narrative amounts to a massive refutation of Ahab's single-mindedness.

Ahab struggles in his own way with philosophical issues. As Ishmael says of his captain, "he strove to pierce the profundity." Ahab himself wonders: "What things real are there, but imponderable thoughts?" Melville may have asked Hawthorne the same question in Liverpool. After announcing the *Pequod's* mission to slay the white whale, Ahab explains his reasons:

> All visible objects, man, are but pasteboard masks. But in each event – in the living act, the undoubted deed – there, some unknown but still reasoning thing put forth the mouldings of its features from behind the unreasoning mask. If man will strike, strike through the mask! How can the prisoner reach outside except by thrusting through the wall? To me, the white whale is the wall, shoved near to me. Sometimes I think there's naught beyond. But 'tis enough. He tasks me; he heaps me; I see in him outrageous strength, with an inscrutable malice sinewing it. That inscrutable thing is chiefly what I hate; and be the white whale agent, or be the white whale principal, I will wreak that hate upon him.

Like Ishmael, Ahab wants to peek beyond the surface, although he too sometimes thinks there is nothing behind it. However, Ahab would not only look behind the mask; he would destroy it if doing so served his aim. Ishmael construes

Ahab's hope for a rematch with Moby Dick as involving more than a desire for vengeance. Ishmael believes that Ahab sees the whale as representing "intangible malignity":

> Small reason was there to doubt, then, that ever since that almost fatal encounter, Ahab had cherished a wild vindictiveness against the whale, all the more fell for that in his frantic morbidness he at last came to identify with him, not only all his bodily woes, but all his intellectual and spiritual exasperations. The White Whale swam before him as the monomaniac incarnation of all those malicious agencies which some deep men feel eating in them, till they are left living on with half a heart and half a lung.

Moody Ishmael may move back and forth between gloomy reflection, quasi-scholarly analysis and jocularity, but morbid Ahab, with half a leg, steadfastly rages at his frustration. His "monomania" sets him apart from Ishmael, who also wants to know but can navigate the sort of uncertainty Ahab cannot. Ahab is willing to tolerate the commercial pursuits that concern Starbuck only so long as they do not interfere with his objective. For Ishmael, the chase is better than the catch, especially if it goes off course, stops, starts again and circles back. While I would not say my old friends from the book club share Ahab's mindset, they could countenance obliterating what confounds them if it meant getting to the end of *Moby-Dick* sooner. The captain also would prefer the straight-to-the point approach to story-telling, if he were the novel-reading type.

Yet Melville made the quest of the narrative far more complex and, to my way of thinking, more interesting than a restrained, refined, and streamlined fishing tale ever could have been. People create, destroy, argue, work, eat, fart, philosophize, die and, yes, even digress, though not necessarily in that order. They at least try to delve beyond the surface world of manners and fussy conventions. Hawthorne found Melville's persistence in reasoning over life's imponderables "strange." That strangeness and its manifestation in a flexible literary method are part of the fascination.

A.J. Liebling also takes the roundabout way for similar reasons, admittedly less ambitiously or intensely than his fellow New Yorker from the century before. Liebling appreciated the value of going off course in pursuit of education. He filled two volumes with essays on boxing, most of which relay what occurred at a particular event – just as *Moby-Dick* depicts a particular whaling voyage – but which often dwell on seemingly ancillary matters. Liebling surrounds discussion of fights with descriptions of visits to boxers' training camps; routes taken to bouts and where he sat once he arrived; conversations with trainers, managers, boxers, reporters, bartenders and fans before and after the main events; what subsequently viewed films confirmed or revealed regarding what he had watched live; and recollections of his earlier experiences with the sport.

Once as I read another boxing enthusiast's book, a fellow New York subway passenger interrupted me. He asked if I knew the author, a trainer and commentator well-known in boxing circles. As it happened, I had been to the writer's house to interview him years before. Did I remember that fighter the autobiographer had guided to the heavyweight championship? Of course I did. Concluding (correctly) that I was not a boxer who would train there regularly, he wondered if I had ever been to one of the local gyms where the boxers' chief second worked with his fighters. Again, yes.

Liebling could fill half a *New Yorker* piece describing random encounters like these. Readers who merely wanted to know the outcome of fights could turn to the daily paper's sports page.

Liebling mixes boxing with other subjects that interest him. The author of *Between Meals* often mentions what he ate.

(He agreed with Ishmael on the importance of eating well.) He intertwines boxing with history and art. For instance, when writing in *The Sweet Science* of the 1955 match between Rocky Marciano and Archie Moore, he speculates that the challenger, after having knocked the champion down but failing to knock him out, "may have thought that perhaps he had not hit Marciano *just* right; the true artist is always prone to self-reproach. He would try again." Liebling relishes the ways those in boxing speak. "In ring language, the verb 'to cut' is often passive in sense," he explains in *A Neutral Corner*. In combining his thoughts on subjects he connects with the sport, he seeks to do more than just cover the fights.

Like Ishmael, Liebling tells tales of learning. "The process of an education, whether that of a candidate for the Presidency or that of a candidate for the heavyweight championship, always interests me," he says in an earlier essay on Marciano also included in *The Sweet Science*. Having followed many fighters over the length of their careers, Liebling charts what they learn over the years. For instance, Marciano succeeded in his quest for the championship by throwing "the kind of punch he wasn't supposed to know how to use." He showed that he'd done his homework.

Looking for such discrepancies between expectations and actual occurrences, Liebling learns lessons from boxing, just as Melville depicts characters, like Ahab, searching for knowledge that might give them an edge. While Liebling expresses curiosity about fighters' fistic educations, he also undertakes his own schooling. He ponders the meaning of Floyd Patterson and Ingemar Johansson's 1959 meeting. Based on prior observations of Johansson, including some dating back to when the fighter was an amateur, Liebling thought the Swede had no chance against Patterson. Johansson's victory leads to ruminations on the deceptive nature of experience, events contradicting perceptions and – again – others' capacity for learning. Liebling had dismissed

Johansson as a limited fighter unable to punch powerfully with his right hand. When a "marvel" of a blow with that fist puts Patterson on the canvas in the first of several knockdowns, Liebling concedes that Johansson displayed "a combination of a rare talent and an acquired knack." In this same essay, "A Reproach to Skeptics" (a title Melville could have used for a chapter in *The Confidence-Man*), Liebling declines to discuss a preliminary bout because it was "without educational value."

Marciano-Moore, 1955

Liebling's affinity for the Melvillean digression can be seen in his piece on Marciano-Moore, in which he likens Moore aiming for the heavyweight championship to Ahab "honing his harpoon for the White Whale." Liebling does describe the fight, of course, but also notes what he had as a post-fight repast after leaving the stadium (a smoked salmon sandwich on an onion roll). Johansson's victory furthered Liebling's education, and Moore's loss also offers lessons. In this instance, Moore may have been the more intelligent and skillful athlete, but he could not withstand the crude but stronger Marciano's relentless onslaught. "It was a crushing defeat for the higher faculties and a lesson in intellectual humility," Liebling writes, "but he had made a hell of a fight."

Of course, *Moby-Dick* also contains a hell of fight. But Ishmael's digressions elevate the novel from being an account of Ahab-White Whale II. As Libeling writes in his musing on Moore: "What would *Moby-Dick* be if Ahab had succeeded? Just another fish story." Impatient readers don't get the full impact of that struggle if they decline to dive into all that surrounds and interrupts it.

DEDICATED WRITERS

Writers deliberately make meaningful use of all their books' pages, including the frequently ignored dedications and acknowledgements. Many readers no doubt routinely flip past these pages. After all, who needs to read dutiful expressions of appreciation to family and friends or profusions of thanks for assistance and support? Yet authors' decisions to thank certain people – especially other writers – can offer insights into what they aim to achieve in main sections of their books.

With dedications, writers pay intellectual or emotional debts, fulfilling real or perceived personal obligations. Patrons, monarchs, editors, parents, spouses, children, readers – all have been so esteemed over the history of the written word. Settling on a dedicatee presents an almost impossible choice, says novelist Edward Docx: "for, aside from the chosen one, every person you hold dear is going to be disappointed." Some try to avoid this problem by mentioning multiple loved ones simultaneously. Jhumpa Lahiri says *The Interpreter of Maladies* is for her parents – and for her sister as well. Moving around the dilemma of whether dedications require "to" or "for," Zadie Smith sent *White Teeth* to her mother and father, but made it for Jimmi Rahman. J.D. Salinger dedicated one book to his mother, another to *New Yorker* editor William Shawn and "split" the dedication to another book between his wife, his children and the amateur reader ("if there is an amateur reader still left in the world"). Thomas Hauser made an even bigger leap from the particular to the general. He dedicated *Muhammad Ali: His Life and Times* to Ali's best friend, photographer Howard Bingham. Hauser dedicated a later book on the boxer more broadly "to everyone who is part of his story." Apparently confident that he would have multiple opportunities for publication, Mark Twain took the route of successive thanks, dedicating one book to his mother, another to his daughters, still another to a friend and so on. The small number of words used in a dedication likely belies the quantity of consideration that went into their selection. Because of the care taken in deciding, Docx says in a *Telegraph* article, dedications offer a large amount of "information" about authors. He provides examples of writers' dedications to figures in the above-named categories (mentioning that Virgil and Horace both cited the same patron) and others (such as "His Royal Highness Prince Posterity," to whom Jonathan Swift pledged one of his works). Still, there may be no more informative dedications than those involving fellow authors.

When writers dedicate their work to particular writers or openly acknowledge other authors, they reveal who supplied their mental furnishings, much as musicians do when they perform other artists' work. When rock groups record cover songs, whether they perform straight recreations or reinvent them to make the tunes distinctively their own, they indicate who matters to them, who played a part in their musical development, how they respond to their predecessors or to the conventions of their genre, and the extent to which they look to other genres for ideas. Whether played respectfully or irreverently, cover songs show where bands are, or think they are, coming from. The same sort of thing happens when writers thank writers or designate their books as being "for" or "to" specific counterparts. This does more than express admiration or reveal influences; it also suggests the existence of a like-minded literary community.

Christopher Hitchens, though he has taken the conventional approach of naming his spouse or children in the front of certain books, frequently chooses other writers for special mention. In doing so, he makes the dedications in his books "reflective of the contents," as novelist Tim Dowling says "the first thing the reader sees after the title" ought to be. Hitchens dedicates *Unacknowledged Legislation*, his 2000 collection of book reviews and literary essays, to Salman Rushdie: "For Salman. As Ever." Another selection of magazine pieces, *Love, Poverty, and War* (2004) is "For Martin Amis."

Hitchens's dedication of *God Is Not Great* (2007) to Ian McEwan fits so well with the book's argument that it could even be said to provide support for it. Hitchens counterposes science and literature, which he celebrates, to religion, which he despises. In the acknowledgements, he says *God Is Not Great* began "to germinate" following conversations with McEwan, but the dedication would be apt even if Hitchens only knew McEwan through his work, which, as Hitchens puts it, "shows an extraordinary ability to elucidate the numinous without conceding anything to the supernatural."

Indeed, several of McEwan's novels deal explicitly with scientific matters, often of a medical nature. His 1997 novel, *Enduring Love,* concerns a science writer's interactions with a pathological person. The definition of de Clerambault syndrome given in the book – "a delusional conviction of being in amorous communication with another person" – gives some sense of its plot. (That the ill individual's "religious convictions are central to his delusions" certainly did not escape Hitchens's notice.) *Saturday*'s characters include a neurosurgeon and a man with Huntington's disease. It has a detailed description of an intricate operation, about which McEwan did extensive research. (In the acknowledgements, he names a neurosurgeon. "It was a privilege to watch this gifted surgeon at work in the theatre

over a period of two years," McEwan writes of Dr. Neil
Kitchen, "and I thank him for his kindness and patience in
taking time...to explain to me the intricacies of his
profession, and the brain, with its countless pathologies.")
One of Edward Mayhew's parents in *On Chesil Beach* is brain-
damaged. While McEwan does not go inside her head the
way Dr. Henry Perowne does with Baxter in *Saturday*, he does
craft a vivid set piece on the son's reaction to learning the
name for his mother's condition, a condition he hadn't even
known she had: "*Brain-damaged*. The term dissolved intimacy,
it coolly measured his mother by a public standard that
everyone could understand. A sudden space began to open
out, not only between Edward and his mother, but also
between himself and his immediate circumstances, and he felt
his own being, the buried core of it he had never attended to
before, come to sudden, hard-edged existence, a glowing
pinpoint that he wanted no one else to know about." Edward
can be seen maturing and moving toward adulthood in an
episode involving his mother's mental deficiencies.

In dramatizing the mechanics of the mind, McEwan
describes the physical and neurological aspects of it – the
brain and all its pathologies – as well as the unique processes
of learning, discovery and decision-making that contribute to
individuals' identities. In a *New York Times* book review,
Jonathan Lethem calls McEwan "the quintessential example
of the recent integration of scientific interest into fiction." In
The Child in Time – a novel Hitchens has quoted in several
places, including *God Is Not Great*, since it appeared in 1987 –
McEwan has a theoretical physicist assert to an author of
books for young readers that writers ought to be fascinated by
science and mine its achievements for their own work:

> "Shakespeare would have grasped wave functions,
> Donne would have understood complimentarity
> and relative time. They would have been excited.
> What richness! They would have plundered this

new science for their imagery. And they would have educated their audiences too. But you arts people, you're not only ignorant of these magnificent things, you're rather proud of knowing nothing."

While it can be tricky to ascribe fictional characters' views to their creators, McEwan's body of work does suggest that he would share this outlook. In a piece of nonfiction in which he voices his belief that consciousness does not survive death, McEwan directly states views on religion in accord with Hitchens's thesis in *God Is Not Great*. "Much damage has been done to thought as well as to persons by those who are certain there is a life – a better, more important life – elsewhere," McEwan writes in his contribution to *What We Believe but Cannot Prove: Today's Leading Thinkers on Science in the Age of Certainty*. His interest in brief spans of consciousness pervades his fiction, where he eagerly combines artistry and scientific inquiry.

Hitchens also examines the ways people use their heads, or fail to. In *Why Orwell Matters* he says another of his favored writers "illustrates that…it matters not what you think, but *how* you think." This distinction reappears in *God Is Not Great*, where he writes of various religious thinkers: "We have nothing much to learn from *what* they thought, but a great deal to learn from *how* they thought." For him, religion represents an "attempt to assert the literal and limited mind over the ironic and inquiring one." Faith can be seen as voluntary brain-damage. He much prefers the sort of skeptical thinking that, using reason and the scientific method, has provided better explanations of "anything important" than any religion ever did. No less important is literature, which "sustains the mind and – since there is no other metaphor – also the soul." He concludes his polemic against religion by calling for "a renewed Enlightenment" based "on the proposition that the proper study of mankind is man, and woman," and depending on both the "study of literature and poetry" and the "pursuit of unfettered scientific inquiry." In other words, he hopes to see more people thinking like Ian McEwan, the embodiment of New Enlightenment values and methods. A more apt dedicatee for *God Is Not Great* probably could not have been found.

Some dedicatory reciprocity can be observed among those in Hitchens's secular pantheon. Rushdie dedicated *Step across This Line*, his 2002 collection of a decade's worth of nonfiction, to Hitchens. Despite this nod to a peer, Rushdie does dedicate other books to relatives, whether by blood or marriage (he says his 2005 novel, *Shalimar the Clown,* is for his grandparents, while 2001's *Fury* is "For Padma"). Amis also finds dedicatees close to home; this has included mentioning his famous-writer father. And one of his books of essays is pledged to a Christopher, among others indicated by first name only. McEwan also seems to prefer a personal approach, inscribing several novels to Annalena, for instance.

Without explicitly discussing dedications, Clive James would seem to endorse Hitchens's practice when he offers this suggestion to writers: "if you have felt gratitude for a fellow artist's life, don't content yourself with telling him personally: say it in public – someone who knows neither of you might take heart." Much of *Cultural Amnesia* can be seen as James expressing precisely this sort of thankful praise. Some of the individuals he writes about are historical figures he knows exclusively through their work, while others he did actually meet.

As it happens, many of Hitchens dedicatees are not simply artists whose work has inspired him; Amis, McEwan and Rushdie are personal friends. One can imagine a dinner party in London or Manhattan where they agreed to put each others' names on pages at the front of their respective books. A 2006 profile in the magazine once edited by one of Salinger's dedicatees does describe Hitchens at a dinner party, but not one with this particular guest list. Ian Parker also relates that the lunch gatherings of the *New Statesman* staff when it included Amis, McEwan and Hitchens as well as poet James Fenton and novelist Julian Barnes, "in which they out-joked each other on matters of sex, literature, and nuclear disarmament, now have the status of literary legend." *The New Yorker* offers no word on whether they planned their future books' dedications.

In any case, more than mutual, intramural appreciation is at play here. Hitchens's dedicating *God Is Not Great* to McEwan makes sense. It potentially contributes to understanding of the book's argument, since McEwan stands as an exemplary intellectual model set in contrast to the sort of thinking Hitchens attacks. Similarly, his friends' choices are not arbitrary. The novelists Amis and Rushdie both dedicate nonfiction works to their friend the journalist and polemicist. (Perhaps McEwan will return the favor to Hitchens in some future compilation of articles.) Further, Rushdie's collection shows him to share Hitchens's views (as well as McEwan's) on subjects such as religion. ("The wrongness of the sacred tales hasn't lessened the zeal of the devout in the least," Rushdie writes. "If anything, the sheer out-of-step zaniness of religion leads the religious to insist ever more stridently on the importance of blind faith." The passage and others like it would not be out of place in *God Is Not Great*.) While Hitchens has made a name for himself with commentary on subjects like religion and politics, he has written book reviews and literary essays throughout his career, which makes Amis presenting a grouping of his reviews to a Christopher I presume to be Hitchens equally apposite. (In the acknowledgments to *The Moronic Inferno*, Amis thanks Barnes, among other writers and editors.) It's easy to see how this group of erudite, independent-minded writers would enjoy each others' company and conversation, even if that dinner party discussion never happened.

Hitchens and the circle of dedicated writers around him perpetuate a simultaneously literary, historical and social tradition with their tributes. Just as Herman Melville famously inscribed *Moby-Dick* to Nathaniel Hawthorne "in token of [his] admiration for his genius," Kingsley Amis, Martin's father, dedicated his best known novel, *Lucky Jim*, to life-long friend and fellow writer Philip Larkin. Hitchens dedicated his book on Orwell to Robert Conquest: "premature anti-fascist, premature anti-Stalinist, poet and mentor, and founder of 'the united front against bullshit'" – a list of attributes and associations to which he could append *confrère* of Larkin and Amis *père*. The practice James recommends and Hitchens extends resonates across generations.

THE FIGHTING LIFE

Aging, social class, race, gender, nationality – writers throughout history have used pugilism in order to show characters dealing with such fundamental matters of human experience. Literature abounds with stories of individuals confronting questions of identity through boxing. While numerous authors have devoted full-length works to examinations of the sport and its cultural significance, others, from Homer and Virgil to Norman Mailer and Philip Roth, have incorporated crucial episodes involving boxing into what would not be explicitly characterized as boxing stories. Boxing contributes in crucial ways to characters' development in Roth's *The Human Stain* and Mailer's *Tough Guys Don't Dance*. Roth also writes about boxing in *Exit Ghost,* where the sport inserts itself in connection with another writer who wrote about boxing, George Plimpton. Roth and Mailer depict boxers and former boxers that resemble those of the Greek and Roman epics, and both writers meaningfully mingle their fictional fighters with historical boxers.

Although closely associated with the sport of boxing, both through his friendships with fighters and through his writing about them, Mailer in his fiction uses boxing in a fairly limited fashion compared to Roth. Mailer's body of work includes numerous nonfiction pieces about boxing and in works such as *The Fight* Mailer closely examines existential themes he connects with the sport. He also peoples his fiction with fighters. When in his novels he provides individuals with boxing backgrounds, he uses the sport as a sort of shorthand to give characters a certain set of defined characteristics and attributes. He does not develop these qualities at great length except insofar as they relate to masculinity. Racial identity and aging recur as related themes secondary to or not completely independent of manliness. In contrast, Roth's treatment of the sport in *The Human Stain*, which includes fully elaborated metaphors as well as resonant historical references, subtly illuminates numerous facets of his protagonist's complex character.

Mailer portrays the narrator of *Tough Guys Don't Dance,* a writer, as sharing his view of writing as a competitive endeavor. "His competitiveness!" Plimpton writes of Mailer in *Shadow Box.* "I had known him for years and marveled at it. It consumed him." Plimpton invariably thought of Mailer and Hemingway as a pair because of their similarities. "I could never think of the two writers without thinking of the competitive streak in both which was so apparent, and without wondering ... if such intensity was a necessary adjunct to one's craft." In *Tough Guys Don't Dance*, Timothy Madden and another writer in Provincetown "needed each other if only to be critical of our contemporaries together.... Our rage against the talent of those who were our age and successful made the marrow of many an evening...." Mailer also makes Madden a former amateur boxer, one who turns to the sport for metaphors. As a journalist, Mailer does the same thing. Writing about the 1968 presidential conventions in *Miami and the Siege of Chicago,* for instance, he invokes the sport when remarking on elusiveness. "To surprise a skillful politician with a question," he observes, "is ... approximately equal in difficulty to hitting a professional boxer with a barroom hook." (Roth similarly likens boxing to another professional activity in *The Humbling* when agent Jerry Oppenheim tells his client Simon Axler that he knows someone who, much like a boxing trainer, can help him regain confidence in his acting ability: "He's a maverick, he's a scrapper, and he'll get you back into contending. He'll put the fight back in you.") Madden compares a kiss to a combination of punches before conceding that that "is not the way to describe a kiss." Drawing on the presumed connection between fighting and expression, he likens a conversation to a boxing match.

Mailer more explicitly links boxing and writing in his nonfiction. According to Joyce Carol Oates, boxing is "our most dramatically 'masculine' sport, and our most dramatically 'self-destructive' sport," and Mailer imbues the sport with both qualities in his writing about it. In *The Spooky Art,* he attributes his lifelong interest in the sport to its resemblance to his profession and its attendant difficulties. (He is not always convincing when describing the mental and physical rigors of writing as akin to those boxers must endure.) "No physical activity is so vain as boxing," he writes in *The Fight,* explaining that a "man gets into the ring to attract admiration. In no sport, therefore, can you be more humiliated." He clearly views writing as entailing similar potential for glory and risk of disgrace. Aging writers and prizefighters late in their careers both "must believe that the work will prove truly important. Or else why suffer the slow self-destruction it will entail?" While the potential for suffering punishment increases with age, the gender aspect persists throughout the lives of fighters and (male) writers.

Mailer maintains a boxing motif throughout *Tough Guys Don't Dance,* and the manliness attributed to the sport echoes statements Mailer elsewhere makes about himself. The novel's title derives from an anecdote involving boxers that Madden's father told him after he lost a Golden Gloves fight. Madden explains what he should have done differently: "My mistake was that I didn't dance.... I should have gone: Stick! Stick! Slide! ... and circled away. Then back with the jab, dance out of range, circle and dance, stick him!" His father responds with a story about mob boss Frank Costello and several professional boxers. After Tony Galento, Tony Canzoneri and Rocky Marciano take turns dancing with Costello's date, the boxers tell the gangster he ought to go out on the floor. "Costello ... shakes his head. 'Tough guys,' he says, 'don't dance.'" Looking back on his father's comment, Madden wonders if there is any more depth to it than it first appears.

> Surely my father had meant something finer than that you held your ground when there was trouble, something finer that doubtless he could not or would not express, but it was there, his code. It could be no less than a vow.

Boxers' virtues have relevance beyond the realm of their sport. Madden's father has "the best will in the world," which helped Madden to become, in a rather tortured circumlocution, "not wholly un-macho." Mailer designates such will power along with ingenuity and strategic thinking as the defining features of a successful fighter's personality when describing the "intellectual content" of fights in his introduction to *Sting Like a Bee,* which former boxer José Torres authored with sportswriter Bert Sugar. As evidence of the style of manliness he learned from his father, Madden points to his ability to "stand up for my friends." In *Miami and the Siege of Chicago,* Mailer writes of wanting to shield Torres (indentified only as "a professional boxer" and one of Mailer's best friends) from possible harm as a reason for avoiding anti-Vietnam war protests.

The Maddens are not the only subscribers to the boxer's tough-guy code. Madden's wife's lover, Bolo Green, also has an amateur boxing background. In addition, Mailer's cast of boxers includes Sergius O'Shaugnessy in the 1959 story "The Time of Her Time" and Stephen Rojack in the 1965 novel *An American Dream.* Although rule-governed, regulated, refereed boxing differs from the raw violence of spontaneous fistfights, Mailer frequently involves erstwhile boxers in such personal confrontations. In both of the earlier works violence is associated with sex. Whereas Madden only tentatively describes a kiss as resembling a flurry of blows, O'Shaugnessy, an ex-Air Force boxer, and Denise Gondelman furiously engage in "a fuck the equivalent of a fifteen round fight." Though Madden fights Spider Nissen and Stoodie, he commits no violence against women. O'Shaugnessy and Gondelman do fight, and she gets in the last punch. Rojack not only confronts Ike "Romeo" Romalozzo, another ex-boxer; he also fights with his wife, whom he strangles to death. Writing of these episodes, Barry H. Leeds says they all involve men whose real battle is with themselves and their own "fears and weaknesses" or, more precisely, fears of weakness. The values of courage and discipline Leeds sees underlying each of these "external manifestation of the true struggle within oneself against the ignoble, ignominious emotions of cowardice and moral sloth" are the values of boxing in Mailer's work.

Invoking the sport's tight association with race and racism in *Tough Guys Don't Dance*, Mailer has Acting Chief of Police Alvin Luther Regency refer to Muhammad Ali by the "slave name" the boxer had rejected long before. "I hate to quote a nigger, but Cassius Clay said it: 'You ain't as dumb as you look,'" Regency tells Madden. Despite never losing in the Golden Gloves, Bolo Green could not pursue a career as a boxer because of one of those fights outside the ring in which policemen fractured his skull. Mailer associates the black boxer with menace – Madden believes he should "mess with him under few circumstances" – but he does not meditate on race to the extent that he does in his nonfiction. In *The Fight*, for instance, he conflates boxing with blackness. By learning about Africa, he suggests, he will not only understand the fight between Ali and George Foreman (another black embodiment of menace) staged in Zaire in 1974. He will also, more importantly, gain insights into the thinking of the black athletes who dominate the sport and, by extension, comprehend blackness itself. He claims an affinity for the view of humans as forces instead of beings that he attributes to the tribes of the Belgian Congo that the Dutch priest Father Tempels chronicled in *Bantu Philosophy*.

> For Heavyweight boxing was almost all black, black as Bantu. So boxing had become another key to revelations of Black, one more key to black emotion, black psychology, black love. Heavyweight boxing might also lead to the room in the underground of the world where Black kings were installed: what was Black emotion, Black psychology, Black love?

However, Mailer immediately confronts a roadblock on his path to racial enlightenment: fighters' psychology. Boxers, he knows, are tricksters. They disguise their intentions. They feint. They set traps. They do not make their thoughts known. For if one fighter can tell what another is thinking, then he know what his opponent plans to do, making deception central to success in the sport.

This aspect of boxing is central to Roth's *The Human Stain*. Like Madden, who fought only one Golden Gloves bout, Coleman Silk in *The Human Stain* also has a relatively short boxing career. However, the sport essentially forms the person Silk becomes – the person he creates and remains long after he left the ring. Boxing supplies Madden with a manly code and a sense of competitiveness that carries over into his career as a writer, but for Roth's character boxing provides even more. Boxing not only reveals to Silk his capacity to be taken for something other than a black man; it also imparts an outlook and cultivates qualities Silk carries with him into his seventies.

Boxing teaches Silk the pleasures and uses of concealment. His immersion in the sport and realization of its mental aspects lead to the decisive moment in the creation of his singular identity. He learns the power of secretiveness.

This discovery happens before he briefly becomes a "Howard Negro," but his time at the all-black college only confirms in him his desire to seize the opportunity for autonomy his boxing experience opened to him. Before he went to the school, Silk had never heard himself called a nigger. Yet he does not take comfort in the "we" of the school. Indeed, he rebels against it. "Overnight the raw I was part of a we with all of the we's overbearing solidity, and he didn't want anything to do with it...." He rejects "the tyranny of the we" in favor of "the raw I with all its agility," and boxing contributed to his becoming "the greatest of the great *pioneers* of the I."

The first "we" Silk discards, and the one he flings away most decisively, is "the Ur of we" otherwise known as family, and boxing starts him moving on the road to what he sees as freedom. When his father discovers that he's been boxing, Silk commits his crucial act of "combative filial defiance." Asked to acknowledge that his father is indeed his father, the teenaged Silk refuses. "No, you're not!" he screams. Later, he tries to persuade his parents of "the glories of boxing," stressing that boxing is not mere fighting motivated by anger, but an orderly sport depending more on thought than on emotion or brute force. While boxing demands thinking, keeping thoughts hidden from opponents is even more important. When exchanging punches with another man, "the guy still could have no idea what you were thinking.... All the answers that you came up with in the ring, you kept to yourself, and when you let the secret out, you let it out through everything *but* your mouth" – virtually the same thing Mailer says in *The Fight*. Roth's character discovers that "power and pleasure were to be found ... in being counterconfessional in the same way you were a counterpuncher." After the disappointment of Howard, he reflects back on the sport's principal lesson: "Self-knowledge but *concealed*. What is as powerful as that?"

Armed with insights attained through boxing, Silk determines to pursue complete "*self*-discovery" in a manner that will permit him to evade the "rigid distinctions between the classes and races sanctified by the church and legitimized by the schools" in mid-twentieth-century America. While still a high school student, he discovers that if he tells no one otherwise, people will think he's Jewish, not "colored." After the funeral of his father just weeks after he left New Jersey for Howard, Silk decides not to return to college. Having decided to lie about his age when filling out navy enlistment forms, he lies about race too. "He could play his skin however he wanted, color himself just as he chose." When, later, this necessitates a final break with surviving family, he again experienced "the power of it as a fighter." He sees repudiating his mother as a test, one for which boxing prepared him. "Throw the punch, do the damage...."

After the birth of his white-looking children, Silk considers revealing his secret to his wife, but lessons learned as a boxer dissuade him from telling her of his blackness. He decides not to shed his mistrust and caution or "to surrender the diligence, the discipline, the taking the measure of every last situation" that he used to navigate through life to that point. Like a boxer, he takes care to protect himself at all times, to never let his guard down. Heeding the internal voice that counsels, "Don't do anything," instead of telling his spouse of his full history, he essentially follows the guidance of the boxing instructor who, on the way to a match, did not tell him to say he was white but only not to mention that he was not. "If nothing comes up," Doc Chizner told him, "you don't bring it up. You're neither one thing or the other." He follows the dictum subsequently with women and with the military: "if nothing comes up, you don't bring it up."

Boxing serves as more than a plot device relating to the light-skinned Silk's decision to live as a man with a Jewish background. When narrator Nathan Zuckerman, before learning this secret, realizes Silk, even at the age of seventy one, has "the physique of someone who would seem to have been a cunning and wily competitor at sports rather than an overpowering one," he notices something about Silk's character as well as his appearance. He spies the slick elusiveness Mailer notices in seasoned boxers. Silk's brother, furious about Coleman deciding to live as someone "more white than the whites," also sees the parallel with boxing: "Coleman was not one of those ex-GIs fighting for integration and equality and civil rights; in Walt's opinion, he was never fighting for anything other than himself. Silky Silk. That's who he fought as, who he fought for...."

Silk becomes Jewish in the same way former heavyweight champion Max Baer did: *strategically*. In *Beyond Glory,* David Margolick notes that Baer's "purported Jewishness" had "considerable commercial consequences in New York" in the 1930s, when "Jews were all over boxing, not just as fighters and fans but as everything in between: promoters, trainers, managers, referees, propagandists, equipment manufacturers, suppliers, chroniclers. No major ethnic group in American history ever so dominated an important sport." In order to appeal to the city's Jewish fight fans, Baer claimed his father was Jewish (despite those who said he was the son of a pig farmer). "Baer was only a 50 per cent Hebrew when he set out for New York," one journalist quipped in 1933. "He only became a 100 per cent when he arrived in Gotham...." Adolf Hitler's rise to power affected attitudes toward boxers. "The grim news from Germany only intensified the pride Jews already took in their fighters, especially when they were taking on Germans," writes Margolick. "So while some Jewish boxers in Germany were fleeing for their lives, Gentile boxers in America were pretending to be Jews." Silk, whom Zuckerman had initially thought of as "one of those crimped-haired Jews of a light yellowish skin pigmentation who possess something of the ambiguous aura of the pale blacks who are sometimes taken for white," pretends to be Jewish for reasons other than financial. When his father first confronts him regarding his surreptitious teenage boxing, Silk explicitly states, "I don't do it for the money." Instead, he does it as part of a strategy in his lifelong "passionate struggle for singularity."

Like Mailer, who mentions Marciano and "Clay" in *Tough Guys Don't Dance,* Roth also refers to famous fighters in *The Human Stain.* Max Schmeling and Joe Louis – boxers whose intertwined histories made a profound impact on the way Americans viewed racial identity in the 1930s – come up in the first conversation Silk has with his parents concerning boxing, which would have occurred during Louis's long reign as champion. When Silk's father tells his son that "if Joe Louis can be knocked cold, Coleman, so can you," he could be expressing concern over more than only the physical dangers of boxing. After Louis lost what Silk refers to as "that first fight" with Schmeling, he learned from the mistake that Schmeling exploited and became what biographer Chris Mead calls "a revolutionary by coincidence" by achieving unprecedented acceptance by white Americans, who were willing to view the boxer as a national representative. Silk's father, a former optician who lost his business during the Depression and resorted to working for the Pennsylvania Railroad in a job where he "had to put up with insults in the dining car and … prejudicial treatment from the company," knows that whatever gains Louis's accomplishments might represent remained precarious. If Louis "exploded the myth of white supremacy," as Mead puts it, he did not end the reality of racism. If "even Joe Louis" could be knocked out, then improvements in blacks' conditions might be equally fragile.

By trading a black identity for a Jewish one, Silk remained among likely admirers of Louis. The fights between Louis and Schmeling made Louis an especially important figure for

American blacks and Jews. Schmeling became immediately and inseparably identified with the Nazis, and Jewish organizations regularly sought to frustrate his opportunities to earn money by boxing in the United States. Many Americans regarded him as "an official representative of Hitler," according to Donald McRae. Prior to his fight with Baer, the Jewish War Veterans, advocates of boycotts against all things associated with the Nazis, sought to have U.S. immigration authorities keep Schmeling out of the country. "That one's for Hitler," Baer said after throwing one of the many forceful punches that led to the tenth-round stoppage of their 1933 bout; Baer wore a Star of David on his trunks during the fight. The Non-Sectarian Anti-Nazi League boycotted German goods in hopes of damaging Hitler's regime and opposed the planned 1937 fight between Schmeling and then-champion James Braddock. That fight ended up never occurring. Instead, Braddock fought and lost to Louis that year.

Although the perception of Schmeling as an avatar of Nazi ideology preceded his fights with Louis, those two fights carried a particularly large symbolic load. Schmeling was "held up by the Nazis as a Superman and exploited for propaganda purposes, especially after he knocked out Joe Louis in 1936," Jeremy Schaap writes in *Cinderella Man*. "The hostility American Jews felt toward Schmeling before the fight only intensified upon seeing the Nazis embrace him afterward," according to Margolick. Photographs of Schmeling socializing with Hitler became popular items for display in New York's garment district. Picketers urging a boycott of the second Louis-Schmeling fight distributed similar pictures. While the Anti-Nazi League could not discourage attendance at the second fight, protesters there handed out fliers explicitly declaring Schmeling as a representative of Nazism. The Nazis promoted the notion that Schmeling, who had won and lost the heavyweight

championship earlier in the decade, would bolster their ideas
of racial supremacy by regaining the title. "Hitler and the
Nazis had helped make Schmeling a national hero," Mead
says. The two Louis-Schmeling bouts, and especially the
second one, "had dramatized Hitler's theories of race and
Aryan superiority as few other events had," writes Mead.

Louis-Schmeling, 1938

"And they revealed Nazi attitudes towards blacks that might
otherwise never have become an issue because there were so
few blacks in Europe."

The 1938 bout is widely regarded as a major turning point
in prevailing American ideas about race. "Rather than
describing the fight as a contest between a Negro and a white
man, as many of them had done only two years before,
newspapers now depicted it as a struggle between an
American and a German," McRae writes in *Heroes without a*

Country. "The American symbolized freedom; the German represented fascism." While Louis's ascension to the heavyweight championship was a source of pride for black Americans, his victory over Schmeling the following year resonated profoundly with Jews. "If only Schmeling's collapse can be taken as a portent of the weakness of Nazism as a whole, our troubles are almost over," the *Jewish Times* opined afterward.

Silk desires what Louis inadvertently achieves: to not be defined exclusively or primarily by racial classification. By becoming "the American" instead of "the Negro" fighter, Louis moved into a broader, less confining category. Silk does not vocally assert an assumed Jewishness (as Baer did). Instead, he quietly lets other people draw their own conclusions based on his appearance. Just as Louis moved from routine identification as the black fighter or the "African" to being called simply the American, Silk would prefer to be neither one race nor another and to be only himself.

Despite the sport's enduring importance to his attitude and activity, Silk fought only four professional bouts and suffered no injuries in his more extensive amateur boxing career. Silk's final fight takes place on a card topped by another actual boxer, Beau Jack. The former lightweight champion, who fought in the 1940s and 1950s and built a record of 83 wins in 112 fights, did have several bouts in New York in the late 1940s, when Silk would have been studying at New York University following his two years in the service. However, Jack's fights at that time happened at Madison Square Garden, not St. Nicholas Arena, where Silk's fights occurred. The Harlem venue did stage boxing events on Mondays during Silk's college days. Jack did fight there, but in 1942, prior to Silk's short stint as a pro. Roth does not put his character on the undercard of a fight that really happened; instead, he names Jack for suggestive reasons. The boxer, like

Silk's father, came from Georgia. Like Silk, he joined the military in 1944, though he entered the army instead of the navy. Perhaps more significantly, Jack is believed to have started fighting in battles royal, according to historian Geoffrey C. Ward, fights like the one Ralph Ellison describes at the start of *Invisible Man.*

Ellison depicts boxing as part of the ritual humiliation of black youngsters. The nameless narrator, invited to give the speech in praise of humility he'd delivered at his high school graduation before "a gathering of the town's leading white citizens," first must participate in a "battle royal." Ten boys equipped with boxing gloves and wearing blindfolds strike wildly at each other. "Everyone fought hysterically. It was complete anarchy. Everybody fought everybody else." Such spectacles were common in southern U.S. cities well into the 1940s, reports Ward. When only two fighters remain in the ring in Ellison's version, they then engage in a conventional boxing match without their eyes covered. During the demeaning "smoker" staged for the amusement of cigar-smoking, whiskey-drinking men who yell things like, "Slug him, black boy! Knock his guts out!" the last two contestants still perform just as the spectators wanted. The narrator hopes to get through the fight so he can move on to what he thinks is the real reason for his presence in the leading hotel's ballroom. "I wanted to deliver my speech more than anything else in the world, because I felt that only these men could judge truly my ability, and now this clown was ruining my chances." The frustrating clown is his opponent, who refuses to take a dive in order to end the fight. "For *them?*" he asks the unyielding Tatlock, who replies, "For *me,* sonofabitch!" Tatlock tries to retain some self-respect by at least fighting with earnest determination, even if that ends up amusing *them.* Tatlock does not openly challenge racial strictures, but instead seeks his individual satisfaction within them, as Silk does in Roth's novel.

After the bout, which *Invisible Man's* narrator loses, the new graduate gives his speech, having to pause periodically to swallow blood flowing from a cut in his mouth. The audience laughs and taunts him throughout. He inadvertently uses a regularly "denounced" phrase including the word "equality" and immediately senses the room's mood shifting into hostility. After explaining that he had made a mistake, he is explicitly reminded, "you've got to know your place at all times."

In addition to naming a veteran of battles royal, Roth echoes the grandfather's dying words in Ellison's novel when he describes Silk's father as meekly saying "Yes, suh" to insulting whites in order to hold on to his despised job. The man on his death-bed at the beginning of *Invisible Man* told the narrator's father,

> "Son, after I'm gone I want you to keep up the good fight. I never told you, but our life is a war and I have been a traitor all my born days, a spy in the enemy's country ever since I give up my gun back in the Reconstruction. Live with your head in the lion's mouth. I want you to overcome 'em with yeses, undermine 'em with grins, agree 'em to death and destruction, let 'em swoller you till they vomit or bust wide open."

If Silk's father uses a similar strategy to that of the grandfather in *Invisible Man,* Silk fights life's war a different way, with different sorts of misdirection and disguise.

A classics professor, Silk told his students that "all of European literature springs from a fight." Although Silk refers to the fight that sets *The Iliad* in motion – the "barroom brawl" between Achilles and Agamemnon "over a woman" – the eight-century B.C.E. epic also includes the formalized violence of boxing. In Book 23, Epeiós and Euryalos fight during funeral games held for Patróklos. As a precursor of Muhammad Ali, Epeiós boasts, "I'm best." In *Cut Time,* Carlo

Rotella, who summarizes the fight as "a one-punch KO," observes that by having the boxer use Ali's signature line, "I am the greatest," some translators make literary influence flow from the present to the past.

The Aeneid, too, features boxing in a similar setting. At the funeral games for his father, in Book 5, Aeneas presides over a fight between the young Dares and the strong, older Entellus. The Trojan Dares, skilled in footwork, dodges blows, one of which Entellus throws with all his power, resulting in his falling to the ground as he "spent his strength upon the wind." Entellus recovers from his fall and furiously pummels Dares, prompting Aeneas to stop the fight. More significant than this anticipatory refutation of Silk's assurance to his mother that boxing is not about anger, the first century B.C.E. epic includes a noteworthy retirement announcement. Entellus declares "here – victor – I lay down my gloves, my art."

The Iliad, "Coleman's favorite book about the ravening spirit of man," also has an old fighter, one who, unlike Entellus, refuses to participate in contests, confessing that he cannot move or punch as fast as he once could. Instead, Nestor says:

> . . . Now let the young
>
> take part in these exertions: I must yield
>
> to slow old age, though in my time I shone
>
> among heroic men.

Despite quitting boxing when still young, Silk hearkens back to the old boxers of antiquity. Near the end of his life he confronts the possibility of having reached "the time if there ever was a time to quit the quarrel." Having rejected the "tyranny of the we" as a young man, he faces the *"tyranny* of propriety" as an old man. "At a certain age, he thought, it is better for one's health not to do what I am about to do." This Nestor-like reflection coincides with his decision to see his nemesis, Delphine Roux, at the college from which he had angrily retired two years before. Refusing to accept what is appropriate and avoid a confrontation with his former colleague, he starts off toward her office, convinced of the rightness of "asserting independently a personal free choice" and expressing his convictions, regardless of propriety. Despite having followed Entellus in retiring from boxing as a winner, he retains the temperament as well as the physique of his younger self (even if, sidetracked by the sight of his mistress among her coworkers, he does not end up at Roux's office).

Mailer similarly suggests his boxers' epical lineage. When heavy-drinking, forgetful Madden in *Tough Guys Don't Dance* realizes Regency's implication in the murders Madden first wondered if he might have committed, the ex-boxer describes the policeman like an exhausted athlete. "Regency sat in his chair the way a fighter sits in his corner after he has taken a terrible beating in the last round." In "The Pugilist at Rest," Thom Jones similarly finds drama in the image of a seated boxer. He describes the Roman statue of the short story's title: "The pugilist is sitting on a rock with his forearms balanced on his thighs…. Besides the deformation on his noble face, there is also the suggestion of weariness and philosophical resignation." Jones describes the figure's musculature, and Mailer also portrays Regency's physical strength though a description of him in a chair earlier in the novel: "he had the ability of many a big powerful man to stow whole packets of unrest in various parts of his body." Madden's father (like Mailer himself) might have held a self-conception similar to that of Ali's literary ancestor Epeiós, but late in life he says he did not live up to his own code. As a younger man he chased the man who shot him, but after several blocks chose to stop at a hospital rather than continue the pursuit. "I didn't have the nerve to go on and catch him," he confesses to his son. He believes he failed a test and that doing so contributed to the cancer decimating his old man's body. Mailer forged a fighter's persona for himself. He "perceived gladiatorial confrontation and violence as a central metaphor for his own artistic and personal struggles for growth, fulfillment, salvation," say Leeds, and he tried to uphold this standard throughout his life, which Roth shows in *Exit Ghost*. Richard Kilman, the freelance journalist hoping to write a sensational biography of Zuckerman's mentor E.I. Lonoff, describes George Plimpton's funeral, where Mailer, "eighty now, both knees shot, walks with two canes, ... but refuses help going up to the pulpit, won't even use one of the canes.... The conquistador is here and the high drama begins. The Twilight of the Gods." Kilman describes Mailer as Entellus without the retirement.

When telling a story about himself in connection with Plimpton and boxing, Zuckerman comments on class more directly than does Silk, who in *The Human Stain* thinks about entrenched class divisions as well as separations by race. The Plimpton Roth's narrator remembers in *Exit Ghost* represents a realm of wealth far removed from anything a Zuckerman ever knew. "George's unlikely manner of speaking ... was [steeped] in the Anglified enunciation and cadences of the monied Protestant hierarchy that reigned over Boston and New York society...." When in *The Human Stain* Zuckerman meets the father of Silk's young lover, Faunia Farley, after her funeral, the writer describes the man's speech in almost identical terms. Decades earlier, Plimpton had offered Zuckerman his "first glimpse of privilege and its vast rewards."

Zuckerman identifies class as Plimpton's underlying impetus for writing about athletic adventures like fighting then-light heavyweight champion Archie Moore in 1959 (which Zuckerman claims he witnessed). "It was the issue of social class that seemed to me the deepest inspiration for his writing so singularly about sports, cagily venturing into situations where he plays at being bereft of his class advantages...." He contrasts Plimpton's participatory journalism with that of George Orwell, noting that where Orwell in *Down and Out in Paris and London* and elsewhere endeavored to see and to describe what life was like for those who had touched bottom by enduring extreme poverty first hand, Plimpton "entered a world no less glamorous than his own, the world of the ruling class of America's transcendent popular culture, the world of professional sports." He claims Plimpton's brilliance lay in "his ability to move across the class line of scrimmage" without becoming "déclassé" the way Orwell had. "Climbing into the ring with Archie Moore he was simply practicing noblese oblige in its most exquisite form," according to Zuckerman. By boxing or competing with other professional athletes, Plimpton did not surrender the status that accompanied his class position; rather, he drew attention to it.

Writing in *Shadow Box* about his fight with Moore and the preparations preceding it, Plimpton emphasizes class issues much as Zuckerman suggests. Before the fight he ate a meal off silver dishes at an elegant club. In sharp contrast, he stresses the grittiness of Stillman's Gym, where the exhibition was staged. "The way these guys like it, the filthier it is, the better," he quotes the proprietor saying of its atmosphere. "Maybe it makes them feel more at home." He mentions that Stillman's was originally opened by millionaires "as a charity mission to bring in kids off the street." Plimpton never would have needed assistance from philanthropists, as his clothing alone makes plain. He records what he wore to the pre-fight weigh-in: a Brooks Brothers suit and a striped regimental tie. Lou Stillman certainly takes coats and ties as class signifiers. When he sees how many spectators wearing them showed up for the bout, he realizes he could have charged for admission. Plimpton says he later heard that Stillman "had tried to recoup what he had missed by charging people, at least those wearing ties, as they left." He also learned of a fabulous, forever-running-late friend who missed the fight, her Rolls Royce having pulled up to the door of the gym after it ended and everyone had left.

Silk refers to Faunia Farley as having led the "fighting life" because of her involvement with abusive men, but the phrase also applies to the biography of the ex-boxer in *The Human Stain* and in other novels. Cunning and secretiveness permeate Silk's struggles in and out of the ring. As in Ellison's *Invisible Man,* the biggest battle in Silk's war involves race. In *Tough Guys Don't Dance,* Madden calls himself as "a compendium of dirty tricks," much as Mailer and Torres designate crafty boxers like Ali. The fighting life for Madden means, in part, trying to live up to his father's idea of manhood, while his competitiveness as a writer illustrates Mailer's notions of the affinity of prizefighting and novel writing. Roth hints at a similar bond between writing and boxing. In *The Human Stain,* Roux thinks of Milan Kundera and her attraction to that writer's "poetically prizefighterish looks." Ernestine, who reveals her brother's secret to Zuckerman after Silk's funeral, later sends the writer an old photograph of "Coleman as the fighting machine" she dubbed "Mr. Determined." Authors might merit the same nickname, for according to Zuckerman, something drives them on their relentless searches to find out everything about their subjects. When Zuckerman, standing at his friend's graveside, resolves to write about Silk and his secret, he views himself as "entering into professional competition with death."

Roth and Mailer know what Homer did about the fighting life: even while maintaining their determination, aging fighters inevitably suffer declining powers. Diminished by cancer and aborted chemotherapy and yielding to what Homer called slow old age, Dougy Madden reconsiders the code he previously imparted in his son. He reveals dreaming of spirits who laugh when he repeats Costello's line. "Then they make me dance all night," he confesses. Assisting his son in the confrontation with Regency, the one that leaves the murderous policeman slumped in his chair like vanquished boxer, revitalizes him in what could be his last fight. Silk cannot satisfactorily extricate himself from the absurdity of being regarded as a racist for having used the word "spooks" to describe students who he had never seen, and who turned out to be black like him. Silk "never once weakened in fighting the false allegation against him." Nevertheless, humiliated and embittered, he cannot avoid falling to "the greatest belittler of them all, which is death." Zuckerman imagines Silk and his mistress "dancing their way stark naked right into a violent death." The Zuckerman of *Exit Ghost* reflects on Plimpton after hearing of his death. In *The Human Stain*, Zuckerman, who like Silk trained to box as a teenager, knows the certain outcome of his fight with death when he begins it in a graveyard.

IS MARTIN AMIS SERIOUS?

Critics snarl and bare their teeth at the sight of a Martin Amis work, and *The Second Plane* brought forth the familiar frothing from many a reviewer's mouth. They insist that he cannot be serious, that he cares too much about attention-grabbing style (which does generate plenty of notice). While it would seem bizarre for them to do so, multiple prominent literary critics suggest that he writes too well and that his devotion to craftsmanship is incompatible with solemnity, gravity or insight. Claiming that Amis's "preening" way of writing diminishes or undermines what he says in his essays, reviews and fiction related to September 11, 2001, many of his detractors end up revealing the extent to which he provokes competitive instincts. Seeking to show their own facility with language and artful evisceration, they try to outshine Amis's authorial flair. They habitually look outside his work for reasons to denounce it, implicating the seriousness of their engagement with his arguments.

Amis provokes reviewers to attack the man as much as his work. Michiko Kakutani makes intense adjectival exertions in *The New York Times*: *The Second Plane*, she says, is "chuckleheaded," "pretentious," "nonsensical," "offensive" "weak, risible and often objectionable." She calls Amis narcissistic, glib and cavalier. Leon Wieseltier, also reviewing for *The New York Times*, says Amis "has a hot, heroic view of himself" and has presented his "simpleton's view of the world" in a "clumsily mixed cocktail of rhetoric and rage." Amis unfolds "obsessions and dubious conclusions," according to Jim Sleeper in the *Los Angeles Times,* and the book is "deeply, sometimes self-indulgently flawed." In *Bookforum,* Michael Tomasky says the book provides evidence that Amis has gone "potty" and now resembles "the embarrassing uncle screaming at the television." Christopher Tayler also sees avuncularity of an unfortunate sort, referring in *The Guardian* to Amis's "crazy-uncle outbursts" and saying "the writings collected here add nothing to his reputation." In *The Times Literary Supplement,* Marjorie Perloff says "Amis's "discourse" in his "off-putting book" displays "self-absorption." She articulates the view of many of her colleagues when she declares that "despite moments of brilliant wordplay...one is hard put to take Amis's elegantly turned sentences seriously."

Reviews like these continue a tradition of unrestrained critical assaults directed at Amis. Reviewers eagerly attacked his 2005 novel *Yellow Dog* with vicious glee. Tibor Fischer in the *London Telegraph* described the novel as "not-knowing-where-to-look bad" and said reading it felt like seeing "your favourite uncle being caught in a school playground, masturbating," thereby kicking off the trend of troublesome-uncle insults other critics subsequently adapted. Although Kakutani ends her review of *The Second Plane* by suggesting "Mr. Amis should stick to writing fiction," she previously found his career as a novelist uneven at best. She said *Yellow Dog* "bears as much relation to Mr. Amis's best fiction as a bad karaoke singer does to Frank Sinatra." Scott McLemee said *Koba the Dread,* one of Amis's earlier nonfiction works, "fails on so many levels as to lend an element of grandeur to its collapse. Without the author's name on the cover, it almost certainly would not have been published."

For anyone seeking a psychological explanation, jealousy offers one possible reason for the undisciplined vigor with which critics try to shred Amis's reputation. McLemee's admission of the power and value of his name certainly hints at this possibility. Adam Kirsch, whose review of *The Second Plane* in the *New York Sun* was one of the more tempered, said Amis "has been the target of much free-floating envy, thanks to his literary pedigree, his undeniable talent, and his precocious success." He recounts the "outrage" provoked in London literary circles by Amis's decision to have extensive dental work done in the mid-1990s. "It wasn't clear whether Mr. Amis's crime was caring too much about his appearance or having the means to do something about it," Kirsch says, but the dentistry symbolized superficiality among deep-thinking gossip mongers.

In addition to his teeth, Amis's work has offered readers ample reason to question his seriousness. In *Time's Arrow,* Amis tells "the story of a man's life backward in time," as he puts it, and the elaborate technique he uses gives the novel the feel of literary gamesmanship rather than serious moral engagement with the historical moment he takes as a subject. Though *Time's Arrow* tells the tale of a Nazi doctor, it is not really about the Holocaust; rather, it simply uses the Holocaust in an artistic experiment that makes the book very stylish but also very shallow. In *Koba the Dread,* Amis objects to Communism principally for aesthetic reasons, which makes him seem very superficial indeed. After quoting Kingsley Amis explaining how no one can abandon belief in creating a just society without some "feelings of disappointment and loss," Martin wonders what his father would have had to write about in the "Just City." He suggests that, in a more perfect world, fiction writers like the Amises might not be sufficiently amused or inspired. They would lack material for their writing. Kirsch sees Amis as suffering from a "chronic inability to realize when he's coming across as a narcissist," which makes him prone to "tone-deafness" in lines like this. He and many other critics see it again in *The Second Plane* when Amis says, "if September 11 had to happen, then I am not at all sorry that it happened in my lifetime."

Regardless of whether *Yellow Dog, Koba the Dread* and other of Amis's efforts deserved the howls of execration that greeted them, *The Second Plane* did not. Though reviewers repeat the same gripes that have long dogged Amis, he handles the tricky balance between aesthetic and moral concerns with greater skill in the 2008 collection than he did in the earlier works even as he stays true to his polysyllabic personal style. If elsewhere he trivialized weighty, historical topics, here his focus on how events affect him and his family is not misplaced. September 11 did happen in his lifetime, after all, and he has every reason to take it personally. In "Terror and Boredom: The Dependent Mind," where he says the age of terror can also be seen as the age of boredom, Amis explains the connection he sees between the terms of that title (which he also puts in the book's subtitle: *September 11: Terror and Boredom*). "When I refer to the age of boredom, I am not thinking of airport queues and subway searches. I mean the global confrontation with the dependent mind." Concerned that too many multicultural relativists make excuses for and compromises with the fundamentalist extremism he calls Islamism, he combines his philosophical objections with his concern for his family in a single, powerful paragraph:

> One way of ending the war on terror would be to capitulate and convert. The transitional period would be a humorless one, no doubt, with stern work to be completed in the city squares, the town centers, and on the village greens. Nevertheless, as the Caliphate is restored in Baghdad, to much joy, the surviving neophytes would soon get used to the voluminous penal code enforced by the Ministry for the Promotion of Virtue and the Suppression of Vice. It would be a world of perfect terror and perfect boredom, and of nothing else – a world with no games, no arts, and no women, a world where the sole entertainment is the public execution. My

> middle daughter, now age nine, still believes in
> imaginary beings (in her case Father Christmas and
> the Tooth Fairy); so she would have that in
> common with her new husband.

Several reviewers suggest that this essay, in which Amis recounts his abandonment of a novella about a terrorist, shows his self-centeredness and superficiality. He equates writing with freedom itself, but, according to Kirsch "reduces his defense of the novelist's freedom to a mere guild concern." Yet, as the passage above clearly shows, the freedom he cares about is not only his own, but also that of his daughter and – as should be obvious – anyone who does not want to live in the dreary prison of the dependent mind that he describes. Though Kakutani calls connecting terrorism and boredom "nonsensical," it really is not so hard to follow Amis's reasoning. (*Harper's* contributing editor Wyatt Mason points out that Saul Bellow – a novelist not regularly dismissed as authoring nonsense – paired "terror" and "boredom" in *Humbolt's Gift*.) In a review of the film, Amis (who dedicates *The Second Plane* to his children), notices something crucial: "When was the last time you boarded an airplane that had no children in it? *United 93* has no children in it. It's hard to defend your imagination from such a reality...." He proceeds to think of what adults would tell children on a plane overtaken my murderous fanatics. In defending imagination and opposing those who would impose boredom by lethal means, Amis cannot be called trivial. Indeed, he could even be called serious.

Several of Amis's determined critics invoke George Orwell in bids to make what they regard as an unfavorable comparison. Tomasky, citing Joshua Micah Marshall, refers to "the Orwell Temptation" of facing "a big choice on a big question." Tayler suggests that Amis falls short in his attempt to respond. Ironically, Wieseltier sandwiches his assertion that Amis "writes about politics and history as if Orwell never lived" between complaints that "Amis's freshness is flat" and his obliviousness to "the damage his virtuosity inflicts upon his urgency." Yet both Orwell and Amis champion the freshness that so rankles Wieseltier. The qualities common to most bad writing that Orwell identifies is in "Politics and the English Language" – "staleness of imagery" and "lack of precision" – are not ones found in Amis's writing. Orwell admires "fresh, arresting" phrases in contrast to "ready-made" ones. He likes "phraseology" that calls up "mental pictures." Although Wieseltier dislikes the "ostentatious" metaphor Amis uses in the opening line of the volume's first essay, it meets Orwell's criterion. "It was the advent of the second plane, sharking in low over the Statue of Liberty: that was the defining moment," Amis writes, skillfully registering the hijacked airliner's transformation into an ominous predator. Wieseltier may only be able to see the prose, but I picture the plane.

In the foreword to *The War against Cliché*, Amis, when describing the reviewer's reliance on the "semi-hard evidence" of quotation, writes lines that would not be out of place in Orwell's essay: "When I dispraise, I am usually quoting clichés. When I praise, I am usually quoting the opposed qualities of freshness, energy and reverberation of voice." Amis may not have the habit of "using the fewest and shortest words that will cover one's meaning," which Orwell encourages. Then again, his summary of the difficulty of formulating a response to the problem of Islamist suicide-mass murder could not be more concise: "We are not dealing in reasons because we are not dealing in reason." While Orwell warns against "pretentious diction," he objects to words "used to dress up simple statements" because they result in "slovenliness and vagueness" – words not applicable to Amis's prose. Amis describes Osama bin Laden as an "omnicidal nullity under the halo of ascetic beatitude," and while it might be possible to use shorter words to describe an intellectually vacant person whose image represents a conviction that almost anyone can be killed for the religious views bin Laden encourages, it cannot be said that Amis uses too many words or is imprecise.

Ending a book review by saying the essayist under consideration has some talent but is no Orwell is akin to a drama critic announcing that a playwright might show some merit but is no Shakespeare. Such statements cannot be disputed – truly, Amis is not Orwell – but they reveal nothing meaningful. Nevertheless, this is precisely what Sleeper does in his *LA Times* assessment of *The Second Plane*. Orwell "remains the better guide to truth about terror" and "told truths less affectedly, in writing clear as a pane of glass," he concludes. In "Why I Write," the essay where he says "good prose is like a window pane," Orwell lists four "great motives for writing," all of which can readily be seen with Amis: sheer egotism, aesthetic enthusiasm, historical impulse and political purpose. With so many reviewers spying pronounced self-love in Amis, no more need be said regarding the first. "I could not do the work of writing a book, or even a long magazine article, if it were not also an aesthetic experience," Orwell says of the second impulse, which Amis obviously shares. The desire to witness and record, "to find out true facts and store them up for the use of posterity," also motivated the writing of the pieces in *The Second Plane*. Regarding the fourth, Orwell writes of a wish to "alter other people's idea of the kind of society that they should strive after," and Amis's efforts in this area ultimately may be what so disturbs at least some of his critics.

Amis's refusal to express immediately classifiable ideas in ready-made phrases arouses animus in those unwilling to do the mental work of closely examining his writing. This explains a misleading move almost all the critics mentioned above make when reviewing *The Second Plane*. Kakutani, Kirsch, Perloff, Tomasky and Tayler repeat or refer to the following remark, which Amis made when interviewed for a 2006 article published in *The Times* of London:

> There's a definite urge – don't you have it? – to say, "The Muslim community will have to suffer until it gets its house in order." What sort of suffering? Not letting them travel. Deportation – further down the road. Curtailing of freedoms. Strip-searching people who look like they're from the Middle East or from Pakistan. . . . Discriminatory stuff, until it hurts the whole community and they start getting tough with their children.

Some reviewers quote the passage in order to put *The Second Plane* in the context of an argument between Amis and critic Terry Eagleton that received significant media attention in England around the time when the book appeared there, but others treat it like a "gotcha" moment that clearly reveals Amis to be a repugnant bigot. Kirsch and Perloff repeat it to explain comments made by Eagleton, who likened Amis to "a British National Party thug." Eagleton also said Amis resembled his father, whom Eagleton called "a racist, anti-Semitic boor, a drink-sodden, self-hating reviler of women, gays and liberals." While he does not apply all these labels to the younger Amis, Eagleton does say "Amis *fils* has certainly learnt more from [his father] than how to turn a shapely phrase." Other critics, siding with Eagleton, rely on the *Times* interview to interpret and disparage *The Second Plane*. Kakutani cites it as indicative of the "offensive ... eruptions of anti-Islamic vituperation" she finds in the book. She does this even though a reporter writing for the same newspaper a month before her review ran put the statement in its crucial context. After reiterating the dust-up with Eagleton in a March 9, 2008, *New York Times* article, Rachael Donadio quotes Amis explaining that he spoke soon after the British government stopped terrorists plotting to blow up airplanes. Rather than "advocating" anything, he was "conversationally describing an urge – an urge that soon wore off." Without revealing that Amis called it a "stupid" statement rather than a firmly held principle, Kakutani presents it as representative of his views. While Tomasky graciously allows that the statement "fairly" does not appear in the book because it was not made in an Amis essay, he insists that it is consistent with those writings. Tayler takes it as typical of Amis's "political consciousness" and places it in the first paragraph of his review.

However, *The Second Plane* cannot accurately be equated with a comment Amis made elsewhere. In an absurd, distorting oversimplification, Tomasky tries to portray Amis as the possessor of a "straight-forwardly right-wing point of view." In the piece Tomasky calls "a rant elegantly turned," Amis calls Islamism and all religion "an embrace of illusion" and worries that responses to "those who use terror" have "shown signs of mass somnambulism and self-hypnosis." He sees this in "the Iraq misadventure" and the "neoconservative 'dogma.'" These are hardly the views of a Bush administration ally. Writing of the impact of illusion on history, Amis writes, "It is always a heavy call on human fortitude to acknowledge that such a thing is happening before our eyes, in broad daylight and full consciousness." He (like Orwell before him) wants to see things clearly. While he sees a need to oppose "illusion in its rawest form: virtuous and murderous fanaticism," nowhere in *The Second Plane* does he advocate deportation or "discriminatory stuff" as the way to combat those committed to illusion. Still, detractors find it easier to dismiss Amis's writing by looking outside it, much as they did by obsessing on his dental work a decade before.

Falling for what could be called the Amis Temptation, Wieseltier tries and fails to out-Amis Amis. Sleeper, who repeatedly violates Orwell's first rule for writing ("Never use a metaphor, simile or other figure of speech which you are used to seeing in print"), says of Wieseltier: "Seldom has a reviewer hoisted himself on his own petard so shamelessly" by impugning Amis's artistry while striving to demonstrate his own. Writing for *Talking Points Memo,* Sleeper says "Wieseltier's review is ... preening and melodramatic, an *opera bouffe* of a literary attack, showing mainly that it takes one to know one." In the *Times,* Wieseltier says Amis "is still busy with the glamorous pursuit of extraordinary sentences" and wonders what "has to happen to shake this slavery to style." Yet Sleeper sees Wieseltier writing sentences mainly "for effect" and thus becoming "the pot [that] calls the kettle black." He lists several examples of "grasps at faux paradoxes" and "telltale, compulsive alliteration" that Wieseltier makes as he "strains for virtuosity." While Wieseltier says Amis "appears to believe that an insult is an analysis," Wieseltier compiles "nearly 2,000 words of insults," by Sleeper's count. When constructing his contumely, Wieseltier invokes the recently deceased. He says *The Second Plane* reminds him of a remark the actor Heath Ledger, who died in early 2008, supposedly made when Philip Seymour Hoffman won an Oscar ("I thought it was for the best acting, not the most acting."). In a more literary vein, he makes this attempt at mordancy: "Pity the writer who wants to be Bellow but is only Mailer." Wieseltier's review appeared in print two and a half weeks after Norman Mailer's public memorial service. Sleeper says Wieseltier "invites us to behold his prose and not his point" in part out of envy.

Whatever their motivation, reviewers condemning Amis can become a bit too fond of their own cleverness. Intending to show critical prowess, they instead appear petty – precisely what they accuse Amis of being. They behave much like Muhammad Ali epigones who demean their opponents but fail to realize that if their challengers really do not deserve to be in the same ring with them then beating them does nothing to bolster their claims to supremacy. If the athlete the braggart is scheduled to fight lacks talent, then what would winning prove? Alternatively, how foolish does the boastful one look if he then loses? If Amis can be so easily dismissed as an intellectual lightweight, why must critics such as Perloff and Kakutani struggle so mightily to diminish him, why do they rely on insults instead of arguments to do so, and why look outside the book to find ways to condemn it? Further, who looks worse if those who try to outdo Amis in expressive verve fall flat? Critics who try to display their earnest seriousness and intellectual skills often end up like the fighter who promises an early knock out victory only to end up unconscious themselves – as clear losers. A writer has certainly made a unique accomplishment if literary critics resort to complaining that he writes too well.

WRITE, REPEAT

The fox knows many things,
but the hedgehog knows one big thing.

— *Archilochus*

"Like many a journalist before and since, Marx was not shy about recycling his best lines," observes journalist, essayist, and reviewer Christopher Hitchens, who could have been describing himself – or a great many writers. The tendency to reuse material might initially look like a journalist's shortcut, but it's one capable of serving a larger purpose. The practice can demonstrate an insistent, ongoing intellectual engagement with certain ideas, or a particular large one. Indeed, journalists join writers of all types in Karl Marx's recycling drive.

Of course, in some cases, reusing material is nothing more than simple corner-cutting. In my first publishing job, with a generator of reference works in the days before the Internet was pervasive, I had to hunt through newspapers, magazine, press releases, government documents and the like for statistics to reproduce in volumes intended for those too lazy to do their own research. While my stint at this particular house did not last long, I spent sufficient time there to notice various news outlets repeating themselves. I remember a state university annually issuing a news release about what Americans consumed over a particular holiday. Each year, a local paper would dutifully run an article on Independence Day hotdog intake. The "news" article parroted the text provided to the paper and wording in both remained virtually unchanged from one year to the next.

However, the kind of recycling that interests me has different, less cynical, motivations, and Hitchens provides examples of these in his books and essays. His writings demonstrate a longstanding interest in a definite menu of subjects and a resolute consistency in his approach to them. After September 11, 2001, after Hitchens's decision the next year to discontinue the column he wrote for *The Nation* for twenty years and – especially – after he vocally supported U.S. military intervention in Iraq the year following, many of his long-time readers thought they saw a change in his thinking. He abandoned the left, former fans of his work said. Indeed, he has referred to his "leftist days" as though they were definitely in the past. However, his regular recycling reveals less of a mental and political shift than those he "betrayed" might like to believe.

Hitchens's response to the famous furor connected with a friend's fiction provides a revealing illustration of meaningful repetition. In 1989 – the year Ayatollah Ruhollah Khomeini of Iran announced a *fatwa* calling for the murder of Salman Rushdie because of the "blasphemous" 1988 novel *The Satanic Verses* – Hitchens announced that he was "Siding with Rushdie," explaining, "One must side with Salman Rushdie not because he is an underdog but because there is no other side to be on." After making that unambiguous assertion, in a review of several books about the Rushdie affair reprinted in 1993's *For the Sake of Argument*, he continued to make the case for uncompromised support for Rushdie and his rights. Summarizing the situation in 2001's *Letters to a Young Contrarian*, Hitchens puts it like this: "Here was an open incitement to murder, accompanied by the offer of a bounty and directed at a writer of fiction who wasn't even a citizen of the said theocracy." He makes a few adjustments when returning to the subject in 2007's *God Is Not Great*: "the theocratic head of a foreign state…publicly offered money, in his own name, to suborn the murder of a novelist who was a citizen of another country." He repeats the identical essential point, with slight variations in phrasing, to stress that there really is only one position to take, and the choice should be obvious to any thinking individual.

One aspect of the Iranian *fatwa* that particularly concerns Hitchens is others' unreasonable responses to it. In his 1989 essay he notes that President George Bush demurred at making a statement about the death threat, saying his concerns were exclusively with attacks "against American interests." He mentions this again ten years later in a review of subsequent developments called "Not Dead Yet," which also appears in 2000's *Unacknowledged Legislation: Writers in the Public Sphere.*

Hitchens gives especial scrutiny to writers' reactions, which leave him desiring much more from those who ought to recognize immediately what is at stake when religious fanatics encourage the killing of authors. In 1989 and 1999, he cites with approval Susan Sontag's response to the first President Bush; she pointed out that protecting the rights "to write, publish, sell, buy and read books free of intimidation" and to fight terrorism historically were regarded as American interests. However, many others disappoint him:

> You would think, perhaps, that when [Rushdie] was assaulted by a theocratic fatwa…, his fellow authors would have rushed to his defense…. But you would have been astonished to see the amount of muttering and hanging back that went on. Had his novel perhaps been 'offensive'? Were the feelings of pious Muslims not to be considered? Was he not asking for trouble?

In "Not Dead Yet," which first appeared in *Black Book* in 1999, Hitchens bemoans the "bizarre" response of several specific writers: "John Le Carré, John Berger, Roald Dahl,

Hugh Trevor-Roper, and others began a sort of auction of defamation in which they accused Rushdie variously of insulting Islam, practicing Western-style cultural colonialism and condescension, and damaging race relations." In *God Is Not Great*, he combines elements of earlier arguments and refines his point: "Some public figures..., such as the Marxist writer John Berger, the Tory historian Hugh Trevor-Roper, and the doyen of espionage authors John Le Carré, also pronounced that Rushdie was the author of his own troubles, and had brought them on himself by 'offending' a great monotheistic religion." Dahl gets dropped from the wall of shame, but those questioning quotation marks remain firmly around variants of the word "offense."

The relentless criticism of religion, far from revolving exclusively around Rushdie, forms part of an effort to encourage skeptical, critical thinking. Hitchens sees the sort of credulity he associates with religious belief as unnecessarily constraining human potential. This leads him again to a point he makes in 2002's *Why Orwell Matters*: "it matters not what you think, but *how* you think." This distinction reappears in *God Is Not Great*, where he says of various religious thinkers: "We have nothing much to learn from *what* they thought, but a great deal to learn from *how* they thought." Giving a sense of the mental maneuvers he prefers, Hitchens often wields Occam's razor. For instance, he mentions the principle of economy that disposes of unnecessary assumptions and needlessly convoluted explanations in *Letters*, in a piece in *For the Sake of Argument* and several times in *God Is Not Great*. In contrast, religion represents an "attempt to assert the literal and limited mind over the ironic and inquiring one." He said in 1989 that the Rushdie *fatwa* signaled "an all-out confrontation between the ironic and the literal mind."

Having taken sides in this intellectual struggle and having committed to doing related mental heavy lifting, Hitchens aims to debunk miracles. The question of miracles has special importance for revealing the fraudulence of man-made religion because "exceptional claims demand exceptional evidence" and "what can be asserted without evidence can also be dismissed without evidence," as he asserts in *God Is Not Great*. Believers reveal themselves unsatisfied with faith alone, or they wouldn't look for signs of a god in the form of unexplainable events, which are in any case invariably explainable without the assumption of a supernatural being.

He exposed the falsehood of a particular miracle claimed in connection with a well-known religious figure long before *God Is Not Great* appeared. But given that work's thesis, how could he not take another look at material included in an earlier, related book, 1995's *The Missionary Position: Mother Teresa in Theory and Practice?* The Vatican invited him to testify regarding the nun's beatification, which makes it hard for him to avoid covering some of the same ground as he did in a 2001 piece about his chance to make the case against Mother Teresa, included in 2004's *Love, Poverty, and War* and revisited in *Letters*.

When Hitchens writes in *God Is Not Great*, "I have been writing this book all my life," he does not exaggerate. Nor did he drop the subject after having laid it out in detail there. The introduction to 2007's *The Portable Atheist*, an anthology he compiled of writings against belief, distills the argument he made in the book-length onslaught issued earlier the same year. Reducing the nearly 300 page attack into just a few pages, he echoes certain lines for which he clearly has a fondness. In both places he describes god as a "man-made concept" that belongs to "the infancy of the species." Despite this, he has little hope for human beings' ability to outgrow it. "Religious faith is, precisely *because* we are still-evolving creatures, ineradicable," he explains in *God Is Not Great*. "It will never die out, or at least not until we get over our fear of death, and of the dark, and of the unknown, and of each other." He presents a variant of the line, including the part about fear of death and the dark, in *The Portable Atheist*. In both books he contemplates religions' paradoxical demand for submission and sacrifice of self-regard while simultaneously encouraging a self-centered belief in personal centrality to a divine plan. He contrasts religion with literature, asserting, as he does in *The Portable Atheist*, that "as a source of ethical reflection and as a mirror in which to see out human dilemmas reflected, the literary tradition is infinitely superior to the childish parables and morality tales, let alone the sanguinary and sectarian admonitions, of the 'holy' books." He says virtually the same thing, using many of the same words, in *God Is Not Great*:

> The serious ethical dilemmas are better handled by Shakespeare and Tolstoy and Schiller and Dostoevsky and George Eliot than in the mythical morality tales of the holy books. Literature, not scripture, sustains the mind and – since there is no other metaphor – also the soul.

Many writers take on a curatorial function, preserving not only their own highly regarded sentences but those of others as well. Hitchens is not shy about regularly reusing other writers' lines (with proper attribution, of course). In a 1988 review of a Noam Chomsky book, Hitchens quotes Ian McEwan's description of observing daytime television audience behavior as "the democrat's pornography" from *The Child in Time*, which was first published the year before. Hitchens finds use for the line again in a 1994 review of an H.L. Mencken biography reprinted in *Unacknowledged Legislation* and yet again in *Letters to a Young Contrarian*. Since the credulous spectators witnessed by the narrator of McEwan's novel allow themselves to be humiliated and manipulated, just as many religious believers do, Hitchens invokes the line again in *God Is Not Great*. (I confess to having previously written about Hitchens and to having quoted some of his solidly carpentered lines. Doing so strikes me as more worthwhile than preserving unappetizing sausage statistics.)

I did not compile these examples to suggest that Hitchens has dined out on the same material for decades. Rather, by returning to certain vital concepts, and episodes illustrating them, he does what he regards as the job of a journalist. As he put it in 1999: "I sometimes can't believe my own good fortune: to have had the chance to defend civilization's essential principle (no more than payback time, really, for someone who makes a living from free speech)...." The right to unhindered expression and the need to combat those who aim to curtail it have been constants during his career. After Rushdie spent the night at Hitchens's apartment, the State Department called Hitchens, informing that he might now be a target of revenge. Thus, when he says, "The theocratic and absolutist side in this war hopes to win it by exporting it here, which in turn means that we have no expectation of staying out of the war, and no right to be neutral in it," he could have been discussing the possibility of terrorists attacking his residence because of Rushdie's visit to it. Instead, he's referring to the need to takes sides against those who would crash airplanes into the Pentagon (not far from his home) and the World Trade Center. The line appeared in his final *Nation* column in the fall of 2002. When he argues, as he does in *God Is Not Great*, that religion is "a menace to civilization" as well as "a threat to human survival" and that "the true believer cannot rest until the whole world bows the knee," it would be hard to find a better supporting example than Rushdie's ordeal.

Besides, it's not as if only the author of *Midnight's Children* and *The Moor's Last Sigh* was affected. When Hitchens writes, with questionable tact, that September 11, 2001, caused him to feel "exhilaration" at the prospect of directly confronting "theocratic barbarism," he echoes the point he made about the journalist's job a dozen years before and has been making for decades. In the same late 2001 *Nation* piece just quoted, he writes: "I realized that if the battle went on until the last day of my life, I would never get bored in prosecuting it to the utmost." In doing so, he essentially repeats himself, and illustrates the sincerity of the statement: it's what he's been saying all along.

Hitchens begins the review of *Dispatches for the New York Tribune: Selected Journalism of Karl Marx* which I cite at the opening by disputing the notion that journalism lacks literary merit. He notes some of the celebrated authors who also were a part of the supposedly disreputable profession, including Charles Dickens, Orwell, Mark Twain and Émile Zola. He does not point out that recycling is not confined to journalistic writing. The type of writers he holds in high esteem also engage in the practice. Novelists, poets, literary critics, academics – they all do it. While Hitchens points out that many fine novelists also wrote journalism, he could have also shown how journalists who generate lines good enough to warrant reconfiguring and repeating do something that oft-heralded literary artists and other writers also do. The realms are connected even among writers without journalistic experience.

Writers of fiction, poetry, criticism – virtually any genre or style – provide countless examples of what Hitchens remarks on in journalism. In a letter touching on his authorial method, P.G. Wodehouse recounts taking the middle of one of his short stories and using it in a novel featuring his Jeeves character. He then devised a replacement section and sold the story with the old beginning and end. Later still, he fashioned another story using the more recent middle part and a new opening and closing.

Wodehouse has plenty of company. Performing a cross-genre hat trick, professor Stephen Greenblatt gave a lecture filled with self-quotations which in turn was published as a magazine article. In his Gordon Gray Lecture on the Craft of

Scholarly Writing, which later appeared in *Harvard Magazine*, he included a complete, previously published essay as well as the opening passages of several others; the talk also incorporated passages from a series of others he was in the midst of preparing at the time he spoke. George Oppen reproduces sizeable chunks of his "A Language of New York" from 1965's *This in Which* in "Of Being Numerous" from the 1968 collection sharing that poem's title. With these pieces, he does not recycle; he reuses: Lines are identical (or almost, having only slight differences in punctuation and spelling). *New Yorker* scribe A.J. Liebling's line about boxing being "joined onto the past like a man's arm to his shoulder" shows up in both of his collections of essays on the sport. He used it in the conclusion to a 1955 piece later republished in *A Neutral Corner* and also worked it into the introduction to *The Sweet Science*, which came out the following year. (And I admit to having found multiple opportunities to use his line on pugilistic history.) E.L. Doctorow's 1984 book of short stories, *Lives of the Poets*, includes one called "The Water Works," which reappears in modified but easily recognizable form as the twenty-fourth chapter of a novel published ten years later. He called that book *The Waterworks*.

Writerly recycling not only plays a part in the process of creating fiction; it also appears in fiction. A writer's repurposing of his own work is one of the causes of Frederick "Bootie" Tubb's disillusionment with his uncle in Claire Messud's *The Emperor's Children*. When Tubb questions Murray Thwaite about his "plagiarism" of earlier articles, the celebrated journalist replies: "Can one plagiarize oneself? Plunder, yes; recycle, certainly; but plagiarize?" He goes further: "If you've worked to find the right words for what you want to say, then surely it would be foolhardy to discard them merely because of some sense of etiquette – some sense that it was rather shabby to repeat yourself." Messud's character essentially restates the sentiment that uninhibited Hitchens expresses.

Clearly, continually circling back to certain subjects, even using similar phrases, need not signal a shortage of intellectual initiative. Any writer with output as prodigious as Wodehouse – he published more than ninety books – would have a hard time not returning to familiar storylines, settings or characters. Not coincidentally, writing itself was the subject of Greenblatt's lecture at Harvard. Whether *The Waterworks* grew out of the similarly named short story predating it or the story struck Doctorow as a detachable part of a then-work-in-progress, or if some other relations exists between the pieces, the author obviously found New York City fertile ground for his imagination throughout his career. It could very well be the case that after penning the earlier sketch he decided that he had still more work to with the dreamscape he'd set down.

Just like Hitchens with McEwan, many wordsmiths of a literary bent repeat others' lines. Virtually every essay Liebling wrote about boxing quotes *Boxiana* by the nineteenth century writer Pierce Egan, whom Liebling dubs "the Edward Gibbon and Sir Thomas Mallory of the old London Prize ring." One of Edward Said's late essay collections, *Reflections on Exile*, demonstrates the expansive range of his interests and the depth of his knowledge. It contains pieces on literature, history, philosophy, politics, film and music. Despite this variety, Said repeatedly cites the same passage from Aimé Césaire: "no race has a monopoly on beauty, or intelligence, or strength, and there is room for everyone at the convocation of conquest." He quotes or paraphrases it half a dozen times in the book, or roughly once every 100 pages. The poet captures his commitment to the struggle against oppression in the named of shared humanity. That guiding idea animates his work and connects his literary and more overtly political essays. Even with the considerable scope of his experience and intellectual concerns, what really mattered could be encapsulated in lines from a single poem, which he returns to with regularity.

Hitchens may cover an extensive array of subjects, but certain core principles govern how he approaches them, and abiding concern for those ideas lenas to their recurrence. Whether he writes about hated politicians like Henry Kissinger or the Clintons or admired authors such as McEwan and Rushdie, Hitchens continually displays a dedication to independent critical thinking. In this respect, he praises Thomas Paine and Thomas Jefferson in *God Is Not Great* and *The Portable Atheist*. Hitchens also wrote books about both of those men. Recycling, then, reveals not a shortage of ideas but which ones concern the writer most. (Although when, in *Thomas Paine's Rights of Man: A Biography*, Hitchens begins two consecutive paragraphs with the words "Paine went on," the effect is clumsy, giving the impression of work completed in a rush.)

The example Hitchens gives of Marx's journalistic recycling relates to the famous line about historical events occurring first as tragedy and than as farce. Marx rehearsed the line, which he adapted from Hegel, during his days as a newspaperman. Since he sought to discern and describe laws governing historical processes, it should not surprise that he would ceaselessly return to and further hone his statements on the subject.

Similarly, given Hitchens's proclivities and enthusiasms, his polemics against weak-mindedness and his celebrations of exemplary thinkers have a reliable predictability. Someone joyfully aware of the "infinite splendors of literature and poetry," as he puts it in *The Portable Atheist*, can be expected to return to those who, for him, best represent such wonders. A relentless critic angered by foolishness and unethical behavior will surely point to instances of it over and over. A *Nation* article from the late 1980s contains a line that could easily have fit into Hitchens's writing nearly twenty years later.

Indeed, it could operate as his personal motto: "One should never miss an opportunity to celebrate the Enlightenment or to mock priestcraft and the worship of mediocre princes and tycoons." His detractors might argue that he became unduly forgiving of certain mediocrities involved in planning and implementing George W. Bush's foreign policies, but the sentence still does encapsulate his technique, even if it can be argued that he grew less skeptical of the use of American military power than he once had been.

Hitchens of course knows that journalists are not the only serial repeaters among writers. He reviewed the collections of Wodehouse's letters where the novelist boasts of selling several variants of the same work. (His review of Marx's *New York Tribune* articles also refers to Wodehouse's *Psmith, Journalist*, a novel about a newspaper characterized by unimaginative repetitiveness and dull familiarity until the protagonist mixes things up.) In a 2003 *Atlantic* article he mentions Evelyn Waugh's tendency to repeat himself, arguing that Waugh's later works do not compare favorably with the earlier ones. The novelist returns to matters addressed previously but does less with them. (Alexander Waugh in *Fathers and Sons*, his "autobiography" of a family of writers, casually mention's his grandfather reusing a published short story as the concluding portion of a later novel.) After charting several similarities between a work from the 1950s and others written before it, Hitchens notes that in most instances cited, "the preceding books phrased it better." He goes on to lament: "Many literary careers are doomed to go on slightly longer than they should, and to outlive the author's original talent."

Foes more concerned with his political positions that the quality of his prose would like to trace a similar sort of decline in his writing, especially if they could contend, as Hitchens does, that inferior writing reflects wrong-headedness. Reflecting on late Waugh (in light of commentary by Orwell), Hitchens sees a direct link between "suspect politics" and "bad writing."

Regardless of whether this is demonstrably true (in connection with either Waugh or Hitchens), the fact of repetition itself cannot be taken as proof of diminishment. Indeed, the example of recycling Alexander Waugh gives concerns a story published in the early 1930s and grafted onto one of Evelyn Waugh's most celebrated efforts, *A Handful of Dust*, which was only the fourth of his many novels. (Conclusively demonstrating my observations about writers' reuse of both their and others' lines, Hitchens reports in both *The Atlantic Monthly* and in an introduction to another novel by the same author that Waugh took the title of this one from a T.S. Eliot poem.)

Instead, authorial recycling suggests that even the foxiest of writers may have something of the hedgehog about them. Some who appear to seize "upon the essence of a vast variety of experiences," as Isaiah Berlin says the fox figuratively does in Archilochus's famous line, might also display hedgehog-like tendencies, subscribing to an "organizing principle" despite the apparent disunity of their multiple pursuits. Having a great deal to say, as the prolific writers discussed above uniformly do, does not necessarily translate into continually saying entirely new things. Ultimately, it might not be so easy to distinguish between the two kinds of "intellectual and artistic" personalities Berlin defines. Further, a propensity to recycle – or plunder – one's own writing is not confined to journalism. The widespread practice brings journalism into the circle of other sorts of writing more readily regarded as art.

GEORGE & ME

When I read about a claim, published several decades after he died, that George Orwell tried to rape someone, it disturbed me. A lot. I am not naïve. I don't expect perfection from anyone, even individuals I hold in high regard. That accomplished writers may have led less than exemplary lives is not news to me. Still, there is something special about Orwell, and something dispiriting about the idea of him attempting such an act. The reports would not have had nearly the same impact on me if it had been about another writer I admire, but Orwell's persona cannot be completely separated from his work. After all, he wrote about himself in several books and essays. The values and ideas he emphasized in the writing have come to be associated with the man. He argued for clear-sightedness and equally clear prose and appeared to demonstrate both. He would not accept lies from the political right or left. He was independent, not beholden to anyone. As biographer D.J. Taylor puts it, "Orwell is, above all, a moral force, a light glinting in the darkness, a way through the murk."

"All your heroes turn out to be assholes," Shooter Jennings sings in one of those country songs about everything turning out wrong. When I read the accusation against Orwell it felt like one of those sad moments. Was Orwell, decency's advocate, merely a fraud?

Certainly, violence was a part of Orwell's life, and some violence, including deadly violence, can be justified. He did try to kill people when fighting in Spain in 1937, and he may have done so. On the Huesca Front, in what Taylor calls "one of the most dangerous episodes of his military career," he threw a bomb at a group of fascists. In *Homage to Catalonia*, Orwell describes fighters for Franco approaching his position with rifles flashing. He saw one Nationalist soldier just twenty yards away. He made what he calls a lucky toss that placed a bomb exactly where he witnessed the gunmen. The explosion caused a "diabolical outcry of screams and groans," he says, and continues, "We had got one of them anyway; I don't know whether he was killed, but certainly he was badly hurt. Poor wretch, poor wretch." In another episode, recalling the bayoneting demonstration given years earlier by his school boxing instructor, a veteran of the unsuccessful 1915 British offensive at Gallipoli, Orwell tried and failed to stab a soldier in Spain who stayed just out of his reach. Later, soon before being shot himself, he fired at other fascists, but could not say for certain whether he hit anyone. Though he felt some "vague sorrow" after lobbing the bomb, his actions, it seems clear, were warranted.

Sometimes, in Orwell's view, those who oppose violence are not on the side of justice and those willing to fight have claims to virtue. In the 1945 essay "Notes on Nationalism," he writes of pacifism,

> The majority of pacifists either belong to obscure religious sects or are simply humanitarians who object to taking life and prefer not to follow their thoughts beyond that point. But there is a minority of intellectual pacifists whose real though unadmitted motive appears to be hatred of western democracy and admiration for totalitarianism. Pacifist propaganda usually boils down to saying that one side is as bad as the other, but if one looks closely at the writings of the younger intellectual pacifists, one finds that they do not by any means express impartial disapproval but are directed almost entirely against Britain and the United

States. Moreover they do not as a rule condemn violence as such, but only violence used in defence of western countries.

This passage seemed exceptionally prescient and was repeated frequently fifty six years after Orwell wrote it, in the days after September 11, 2001. In Orwell's time, violence against Franco and Hitler was absolutely necessary; in the same vein, supporters of military action against al-Qaeda and the Taliban found Orwell's comments about pacifism and the need to fight especially appropriate.

In these works, however, Orwell discusses a completely different type of violence than rape, which belongs in another category altogether. I do not find Orwell's conduct during the Spanish Civil War morally troubling; the possibility that he might have come close to violating a woman, however, troubles me a great deal.

Perhaps because of the striking relevance of the lines quoted above or because of the renewed attention paid to Orwell as the 100th anniversary of his birth approached, I read a great deal of his published work – all of it, in fact – after September 11. During the next three years, I read or reread every one of his books. My first experience with Orwell had been in seventh grade, when *Animal Farm* was assigned reading: I still have that copy with my name written on it. I read *Nineteen Eighty-Four* when I was in college, just a few years after 1984. And eventually I found my way to his better-known essays (the brick-shaped Everyman's Library edition of his essays stayed with me for a several-month stretch, and it remains a book that I frequently revisit), all his novels, and his nonfictional work, including his account of his experiences in Spain.

To a great extent it was *Homage to Catalonia* – his story of "being in some degree disillusioned" in Spain – that helped me cut through the political confusions that came about after September 2001 and helped me understand one of the "dreariest effects" that the war taught Orwell, namely, "that the Left-wing press is every bit as spurious and dishonest as that of the Right." When I finally read Orwell's version of this realization, I recognized the willingness of committed activists, regardless of their politics, to lie in the apparent belief that, despite all preceding history, corrupt means will this time around lead to just ends. Orwell rejected that sort of delusional rationalizing and set out instead to say what he saw without tailoring his writing to suit anyone's ideological aims. He believed a book should be assessed on its merits, not according to political expediency (as he explained in a 1945 preface for *Animal Farm*). While he ended up with mostly "evil" memories of the "disaster" in Spain, his "belief in the decency of human beings" nevertheless increased. To my mind, this indicates a strong measure of rare intellectual and moral courage – not the sort of qualities associated with attempted rapists.

I first learned of the accusation of rape from a review of a collection of Orwell's newspaper columns. Writing in *The New York Review of Books*, Frank Kermode mentions it in passing, citing another critic's article in another publication before quickly moving on to the book under examination.

Shocked by the suggestion, which contradicted so much of what I believed about Orwell, I needed to know more. A few sentences in a piece about something else were not enough. Did I merely want confirmation of my suspicion that something was wrong with the claim of an attempted rape? Was I simply in a condition of denial? I decided to follow what I took to be Orwell's example as an author. In the 1946 essay "Why I Write" he describes his "power of facing unpleasant facts," and I vowed that I would confront the facts no matter how disturbing they might be. The truth, not some consoling illusion, mattered. If he really was not the exemplar I had thought, I wanted to know it.

I turned next to the article to which Kermode referred. In the *Times Literary Supplement*, Gordon Bowker, the author of *George Orwell*, one of the Orwell biographies that appeared around the centennial of his birth, said the accusation seemed believable. He wrote that the scenario outlined by a relative of one of Orwell's childhood friends fit with his understanding of the writer's character and history. Decades earlier, Jacintha Buddicom, whom Orwell befriended when he was young Eric Blair, had written a memoir called *Eric & Us* in which she recalled with evident fondness their shared friendship in the 1920s. Now one of her cousins, Dione Venables, claimed that previously unstudied family letters revealed that he had pounced on Buddicom, resulting in bruises, torn clothing, and tears, but had stopped somewhere short of committing rape. Venables composed a postscript detailing this for the 2006 reissue of *Eric & Us*.

My copy of *Eric & Us* had to be shipped from the United Kingdom and I waited with both anticipation and dread for it to arrive so I could finally see for myself what it actually said. In the meantime, I immersed myself in all things Orwell, reading about him, revisiting his work, comparing what others said about particular passages to my own interpretation. I decided to read the biography by the person who said the account of the assault struck him as plausible. In addition to reading Bowker's biography, I returned to Jeffrey Meyers's work, *Orwell: Wintry Conscience of a Generation*. I read D.J. Taylor's *Orwell: The Life*, published in 2003. I looked again into Christopher Hitchens's *Why Orwell Matters* (with its section on "difficulties with girls"). And I again pored over Orwell's autobiographical work, particularly with an eye to discerning his attitudes about with women.

Was I going overboard with all of this? I certainly was dedicating a great deal of time to scrutinizing the writer and his experiences with women, even though I knew from the beginning that I would never be able to settle the matter conclusively. With no forensic evidence, no witnesses and no way to question any of those directly involved, there could be no way to know for certain whether George Orwell had forced himself upon Jacintha Buddicom.

When my copy of *Eric & Us* showed up, I quickly saw that Venables's postscript suffers from serious shortcomings. Characteristically, it is Orwell, who set great store by the act of witnessing, who anticipates the main problem bedeviling the appendix to Buddicom's memoir. More than once in *Homage to Catalonia*, he mentions that he is documenting what he saw with his own eyes. He also readily admits that his first-person observation does not give his book anything like an exhaustive history of the events he witnessed. He states, "It will never be possible to get a completely accurate and unbiased account of the Barcelona fighting, because the necessary records do not exist." Before I read her account – before I saw it firsthand, that is – I had assumed that Venables would have something definite to point at to support the suggestion of an attempted rape. She doesn't. Instead, she turns out to be an unreliable non-eyewitness multiple steps removed from the incident at the center of her revelation. Jacintha Buddicom's sister, Guinever Buddicom, told Venables that she had "had discovered a furious letter from Jacintha to Eric, telling him of her disgust and shock that he should try and FORCE her to let him make love to her." However, Guinever had burned the letter. Consequently, Venables (and the capital letters for emphasis can only be hers) relies on a verbal reconstruction of a letter that had been set ablaze more than a dozen years before she reported its contents on the basis of admittedly "hazy" recollections attributed to Jacintha Buddicom's younger sister. Venables goes on to assert that Orwell attempted to "make SERIOUS love to Jacintha" by holding her down and bruising her in the process. Although Bowker and Kermode baldly state that in her postscript Venables accuses Orwell of attempted rape,

Venables does write that Guinever did not think "it sounded as though Eric had raped" Jacintha, since "there was a reference to Jacintha screaming at Eric to stop – and he had." Still, Venables gives the impression that he tried to rape her but then relented.

Even if Venables immediately transcribed what Guinever Buddicom said to her about this in 1993, this leaves ample room for error. The conversation between Venables and Guinever occurred seventy-two years after the alleged incident. She cannot quote from the non-surviving letter, which no one else can examine. Guinever, who died in 2003, can answer no questions about it. Venables is vague about how much of the account was taken from the recollection of the gist of the letter and how much came from its burner's independent memories of the alleged incident. After September 4, 1921 (the date on the letter, according to Venables), Orwell continued to spend time with Jacintha's siblings, but she "made herself scarce" whenever he was around. However, in *Eric & Us*, Jacintha Buddicom refers to a long walk with Orwell in 1922 as well as other meetings. Although documents revealing previously unknown aspects of Orwell's life and personality may appear (perhaps including those Guinever did not destroy), a full, disinterested biography remains unlikely – and for the identical reasons Orwell addressed concerning the history of the Spanish Civil War.

Bowker's willingness to deem Venables's claims credible looked to me like it rested on flawed reasoning – his thorough biography showed close attention to detail, but he seemed less than rigorous in his reading of this postscript. He fails either to notice or to mention that the key document Venables refers to does not exist. In the *Times Literary Supplement*, he states that a "draft letter to Eric, dated September 21, 1921, discovered after Jacintha's death, shows that their friendship was broken off when the eighteen-year-old, six-foot-four Eric pounced on the barely five-foot Jacintha and attempted to rape her." No one knows what the letter "shows." Bowker neglects to mention that Venables depends on Guinever Buddicom's reiteration of the contents of an epistle she obliterated. (And he gets the date wrong.) He also knows, as his own biography makes plain, that contact between the two continued for another year or so until Orwell moved from England to Burma as a member of Imperial Indian Police.

In his biography, Bowker finds Orwell's sexual proclivities in the words of fictional characters, offering selective and superficial readings of passages from the fiction as though this could offer direct access to the author's mind. To cite just one example, Bowker takes Gordon Comstock's fantasizing in *Keep the Aspidistra Flying* of satisfying sexual longings the way beasts do as a parallel to what Bowker calls Orwell's characteristic "pounce." He highlights this passage:

> This woman business! What a bore it is! What a pity we can't cut it right out, or at least be like the animals – minutes of ferocious lust and months of icy chastity. Take a cock pheasant, for example. He jumps up on the hens' backs without so much as a with your leave or by your leave. And no sooner is it over than the whole subject is out of his mind. He hardly even notices his hens any longer; he ignores them, or simply pecks them if they come too near his food. He is not called upon to support his offspring, either. Lucky pheasant! How different from the lord of creation, always on the hop between his memory and his conscience!

Comstock's envy of the directness of animals, it could be argued, speaks to his wish that he could ignore the conventions of respectable human conduct, as well as decency itself, and commit rape. Yet fiction is not always thinly disguised autobiography, and the problem with conflating them can be seen when you try to attribute Comstock's admiration of cock pheasants to Orwell. Orwell was very fond of children. He despaired at the thought of his possible infertility and eagerly adopted a son, Richard. No one familiar with this side of Orwell – and Bowker mentions it in his biography – would believe Orwell shares Comstock's envy of a male animals' freedom from having to support offspring. But if one can point to one part of a paragraph as representative of the writer's actual outlook but conveniently ignore another part, then this method of teasing out a person's real beliefs is spotty and unreliable at best.

Kermode also takes a too casual approach to some basic facts, writing, for example, that "a memoir has been published," suggesting that the book itself, rather than only the postscript, is new. Seemingly using only Bowker's article, and not Venables's actual text, Kermode also says Orwell "tried to rape" Jacintha, not conveying Guinever's observation that he stopped when he was told to stop.

I fully recognize that Orwell does not come off well if looked at exclusively in terms of sexual politics. His behavior could be quite shabby, his attitude toward women rather poor. His works supply ample ammunition for those who regard him as sexist. His interactions with women included several desperate marriage proposals, numerous awkward passes at women who found him unattractive, a great deal of self-pity, and unfaithfulness to his first wife. Nevertheless, Orwell did display a willingness to challenge prevailing prejudices. After a close look at what has been written by and about him, I am not convinced that his behavior with Buddicom can accurately be called "rape" or "near-rape."

Although the far-from-convincing suggestion of attempted rape and the less than scrupulous handling of it in journalist reports persuaded me that wholesale reevaluation of Orwell's work and reconsideration of its enduring value would be unnecessary, I cannot call the journey to this conclusion an enjoyable one. I felt like my literary studies degenerated to the point that they started to resemble a lawyer's efforts to discredit someone on the stand. Investigating novels, essays, biographies and book reviews for what they might reveal about an author's sex life and whether they support declaring the writer a sex criminal is exactly as unappetizing as it sounds. I believed, and still believe, that scrutinizing literature with a predetermined interest in specific issues like sex or politics distorts a reader's perspective, exaggerates certain aspects of books and twists texts to fit particular prejudices. Kermode hints at a close connection between Orwell's biography and his method of expression that offers avenues for just such misreading. He allows for the possibility of attempted rape because of Orwell's familiarity with violence, which had "inevitably been part of his job" in Burma. Kermode also says that "in later life this quiet man did express violent political opinions," as if that might signal a propensity to sexual violence. When I was in graduate school (right around the time Guinever Buddicom and Venables discussed the missing letter), I felt like too much criticism took the form of fatuous disputes over an artist's value based on judgments of the correctness of his (actual or presumed) commitments, and Orwell obviously lost points in such debates. No one would mistake him for a feminist, but I did not want my reading of his work to revolve only around such matters or to ponder whether fierce criticism signaled a capacity for physical attacks.

Everyone has multiple sides and qualities, some attractive, some less so, and Orwell is certainly no exception, as reading biographies of him makes plain. I still think it is important to look at all those aspects, whether positive or negative. In "Notes on Nationalism," Orwell writes, "Indifference to objective truth is encouraged by the sealing off of one part of the world from another, which makes its harder and harder to discover what is actually happening." He earned a reputation for his commitment to belief in the existence of objective truth and his efforts to learn and reveal it. He also proved himself willing to fight, literally and with a defensible sort of violence, for what he believed. One of the things he believed in was decency. Arguing for decency does not necessarily mean embodying it, of course. While it is certainly possible to point to sentences in various works as evidence of misogyny, it is also easy to find repeated insistence on the need and human capacity for decent behavior. There is also evidence that he tried to meet that standard. Looking only at certain elements of his writing or his biography obscures the truth of his achievements, I think, making it more difficult to recognize and appreciate what he really did.

One thing Orwell did for me was provide a model for the craft of nonfiction writing that I could emulate. *Nineteen Eighty-Four* may be nearly bullet-proof, and *Animal Farm* is exceedingly clever and expertly executed, but it's really in his essays, criticism, and other nonfiction that I think Orwell achieves mastery. I do not mean I try to mimic his style, and I do not flatter myself that I generate comparably clear prose. But I do share his commitment to taking care with facts and striving not to mislead. I try to avoid making claims I cannot support with evidence. I also recognize the inevitability of failure in reaching complete truth, due to the inherent difficulty of doing so as well as my own limitations. The drive to see the truth – having the stomach to face experiences directly and the determination to describe them accurately – does not automatically lead to a complete, precise record of what occurred. The hard work happens here. Orwell fully recognized his own lack of objectivity and the possibility of errors infecting his telling of what he saw. Near the end of *Homage to Catalonia*, he writes:

> I hope the account I have given is not too misleading. I believe that on such issues as this no one is or can be completely truthful. It is difficult to be certain about anything except what you have seen with your own eyes, and consciously or unconsciously everyone writes as a partisan.... [B]eware of my partisanship, my mistakes of fact and the distortion inevitably caused by my having

seen only one corner of events. And beware of
exactly the same things when you read any other
book on this period of the Spanish war.

These warnings obviously apply to writing about events other
than the one Orwell covers in that particular work. That
willingness to examine matters closely even while knowing
and acknowledging the elusiveness of truth makes Orwell an
exemplary figure for any honest essayist.

Traveling the path Orwell maps means taking seriously
troubling assertions like those Venables raises. I endeavored to
do so. Still, following as best I can in his footsteps, I admit
that, as an admirer of Orwell, I too write as a partisan,
someone who takes sides based on his understanding of the
facts. I find myself an uncomfortable one, however, one
unsure if he achieves the clear-sightedness he prizes. This
seems appropriate somehow.

With each victory, the winner reduces his world of rivals by one, believing that the universe now sits in a more manageable state of affairs.

– Wil Haygood
Sweet Thunder:
The Life and Times of Sugar Ray Robinson (2009)

PART IV

FIGHTING INSIDE

INK

I knew the other car was going to hit us. As we entered the intersection, I could see that the car approaching ours to my right was not going to stop. Slamming on the brakes would not have kept us out of the way of the oncoming vehicle; it would have put us dead center before it. I made an instinctive decision to accelerate in the hopes that the stop-sign-disregarding driver speeding toward us would not crash directly into the area where my wife, Nancy, was sitting. When the other car struck ours, connecting just behind the front door on the passenger side, it did so with enough force to spin the car around nearly 360 degrees. When we stopped turning, I noticed that the gear shift lever was twisted on its stem. I must have had my right hand resting on it, tensed my grip on it in anticipation of impact, and wrenched it about when the car started rocking and revolving in a screeching, clattering circle.

On realizing that I was registering the condition of the off-kilter lever handle – that I could both be aware of such an irrelevant thing and be conscious of that awareness – I knew I was whole and unhurt. I turned to see Nancy's condition. Jolted sideways, she had hit her head on the car-door window, which was shattered. However, she was conscious and no blood had been spilled.

I know I called a tow truck to haul away the car, which I later learned had been totaled. At the time, in the mid-1990s, I was commuting to a job in Ann Arbor, Michigan, about a 45-minute drive away from our apartment in Detroit's Cass

Corridor area. I had been driving a well-worn Ford Escort until my parents bought themselves a new car and gave me the more substantial, if equally old, German sedan that we were riding in on the day of the crash. In the glove compartment of the aging Escort I'd kept a small notebook with telephone numbers of repair garages along the stretch of Interstate-94 I that regularly traveled in case the raggedy two-door broke down between work and home. When I switched to the hand-me-down, I'd put the booklet in the four-door along with my seldom-used cellular phone. I hadn't had to call any of the emergency phone numbers until that day.

I don't remember if I called the ambulance. Someone did. Maybe it was one of the electric company workers who had come out of their nearby building to witness the aftermath of the accident. Perhaps it was one of the police officers who eventually arrived. The emergency medical technicians who responded asked Nancy a series of questions and then persuaded us that she should go to emergency room to be examined and observed.

The physical injuries, a concussion and a sore neck, passed with time. But the incident did have long-lasting effects.

I immediately returned to the road. I had no choice: I had to go to work. In order to do so, I started driving what so far has turned out to be the only new car I've ever purchased. Nancy walked to work, and was an automobile passenger only infrequently. Riding in cars became extremely stressful for her. Doing so involved much clutching of the door handle and pressing a phantom passenger-side brake pedal. Although our accident occurred in the city, where roads carrying traffic moving at varying speeds bisect each other, creating ample opportunities for things to go awry, freeway driving was especially hard on Nancy after our accident. Other cars speeding in such close proximity was nerve-disrupting. She hated the experience. I was able to resume car travel without thinking about the accident, but the possibility of another one was always at the forefront of her mind whenever transported by automobile. It would be inaccurate to call her feelings phobic, given the frequency of serious injuries and fatalities from automobile accidents in the United States. In the same year as our wreck, close to 3.5 million people were injured and almost 42,000 were killed in motor vehicle crashes, according to the National Highway Traffic Safety Administration.

We did not hold on to the new car for long.

***

Jaguars are the pound-for-pound strongest animals. Sportswriters regularly use that phrase, "pound-for-pound," to compare boxers of different weight classes in efforts to determine who is the compleat pugilist. A superb welterweight might not be able to prevail against a plodding heavyweight who outweighs him by a hundred pounds, but if size could magically be removed from the key factors in a boxing contest – all-around talent, skills, drive, quickness, toughness, conditioning, will – the smaller athlete would be the certain victor if he's truly the best pound-for-pound. Jaguars might not grow as big as lions or tigers. They might not be able to run as fast as leopards. However, they are more muscular and stronger than leopards, and about twice the size. A male jaguar can grow to be eight feet long and weigh nearly 300 pounds. Additionally, jaguars are decent swimmers and adaptable to various terrains. When all their characteristics are considered, jaguars deserve special notice for their power. And for their fierceness.

Jaguars have a distinctive style of killing their prey, which can include virtually any other creature, since jaguars eat mammals, reptiles and fish. While other large cats rely on throat holds to strangle other beasts, jaguars can kill with a single bite through the neck – or right through the skull. One theory of the etymology of their name is that it derives from the word used by the Guarani Indians of the Amazon Basin in Brazil: *yaguara*, meaning an animal that can kill with one leap.

In his memoir *Somebody's Gotta Tell It*, Jack Newfield outlines what he calls the "Joe Frazier method" of journalism. For him, the boxer "represented discipline, tenacity, courage, and maximizing whatever talent God gives you." These qualities can be used as the foundation for an approach to writing: "keep coming forward. Don't get discouraged. Be relentless. Don't stop moving your hands. Break the others guy's will." Such an approach could also be seen as jaguar-like, since the cats display all the qualities Newfield describes.

Jaguars "must be among the most nocturnal of all felines" and "are more likely to be heard than seen," say the photographers Edwin and Peggy Bauer, who did manage to see a few and capture their images on film. For a long period, jaguars' invisibility in the United States had less to do with their stealth or preference for moving at night than with their actual absence. However, after a long period of not being seen in the country, jaguars were sighted in the Southwest in the early years of the twenty-first century. Apparently, some male cats wander back and forth between northern Mexico and places such as Arizona, possibly using the same routes frequented by smugglers and drug traffickers.

A man who glimpsed one of the rarely seen cats said he could tell that it was not afraid of anything.

Thus, in addition to embodying strength, determination, relentlessness, elusiveness and cunning, jaguars also represent resilience and fearlessness.

***

The women in the 007 movies – the so-called Bond girls – may be widely regarded as eye candy or as accessories to the dashing masculine spy character created by Ian Fleming, but some of the movies, even early ones, do have some strong female characters. It's not necessary to argue for a feminist interpretation of the films to see that not all the women in them were demure or subservient. Certainly, there are damsel-in-distress scenarios in the films, but there are also women who are James Bond's quick-thinking equivalents. *In The Spy Who Loved Me*, Anya Amasova, codename XXX, is the Russian counterpart to Bond and the KGB's best agent. In *Thunderball*, it's Domino who kills the arch-villain (who also had been her lover-turned-tormentor). The title character of *Octopussy* runs an all-female band of smugglers, which joins with Bond to destroy his foe, who had also betrayed the character played by Maud Adams. Earlier, in *Goldfinger*, a woman leads an all-female group of pilots. Regarding her role in *Die Another Day*, actress Halle Berry says, "She was very intelligent. She was Bond's equal... She had to save him a few times in the movie. Bond and Jinx had a great partnership."

Some people, including another former Bond girl, do regard the female characters as embodiments of admirable qualities that make them symbols of strength worth claiming for feminism. The Bond women are "lasting icons of feminine strength, beauty and resilience," writes Maryam D'Abo in *Bond Girls Are Forever*, a coffee-table book she co-authored. D'Abo also produced a documentary of the same name and co-starred in the 1987 Bond film *The Living Daylights*.

***

Not long after our car wreck, we left Detroit and lived in cities where owning an automobile would not only be unnecessary but would also be an expensive hassle rather than a convenience. I got an editing job with a specialized agency of the United Nations and we moved Geneva, Switzerland.

Someone I met there described the country as one full-size train set, and it is easy to move through the mountains and valleys without driving. We found Geneva to have an easy-to-use, reliable system of trams and buses that made it simple to get around (unless it was late at night, when there was no service). From there, we moved to New York, where we quickly adapted to subway travel from our apartment in Brooklyn to our offices in Manhattan. Once we determined that we would not return to Detroit, we arranged to sell our long-garaged car.

Where we decided to live in Brooklyn, a person can easily walk to shops or restaurants. Bookstores, the bank, the grocery store, the dry cleaner, the hardware store – all are down the block, around the corner, just a few minutes away. After relocating to New York, we would turn down rides occasionally offered by friends who happened to drive. In most cases, we judged, it was easier, and probably quicker, to take the train. We've never minded walking, so when we've traveled to other cities, we tended to explore on foot as much as possible.

While yellow cabs crowd the streets of Manhattan, car-less Brooklyn residents typically turn to dispatched car services on those occasions when they need a ride. For us, such a need did not arise very often. Most likely, arranging to be picked up for such a trip meant heading to an airport. About once a year or so that would mean a trip to see my parents back in Detroit, where car travel is unavoidable.

Getting from the airport to my parents' house and then going from there to anywhere else we might visit while in town – every move involves car trips. In northwestern Detroit, where my family lives, and in much of the city, the sort of pedestrianism we knew in Geneva and grew to take for granted in Brooklyn simply is not an option. Even after many of the factories where Fords and Chevrolets and Chryslers were once manufactured closed down, the Motor City remained all about the automobile.

Nancy dreaded these trips. If she were ever to make a movie in which a character had to endure her every conceivable aversion simultaneously, Nancy could draw on recollections of being wedged in the backseat, and every uncomfortable ride would involve both freeway travel and traversing Detroit's rough, pot-holed roads.

Cinema of a different sort gave us an idea of how to stop the ceaseless repetition of the unpleasant vehicular scenes flickering on her mental movie screen. In the Bond movies, women put up with exceptionally trying car trips. They might not be trapped between in-laws, but they do have high-speed chases, ride in cars that operate under water, have giants with sharp metal teeth rip their vehicle apart when they try to escape and ride motorcycles over roof tops. And they handle it all with aplomb.

Before one of our annual trips to Detroit, Nancy decided to approach matters like one of the poised and resourceful Bond characters. She would not be made miserable by contemplation of possible catastrophes. She would be fearless. In a moment of simultaneous seriousness and silliness, we tried to come up with a Bond-girl-style name (for private use by the two of us) to go with the new outlook. Porn-star-like monikers such as Honey Ryder, Pussy Galore, Holly Goodhead, and Xenia Onatopp obviously would not serve our purpose. They did not provide the model to follow. Nancy's real name does not lend itself to a nickname the way Dominique can be made into Domino. We wanted one that not only suggested the cinematic source of inspiration but also reflected the characteristics she wanted to cultivate. Eventually we came up with one: Jaguar.

The idea worked. As it turned out, the first trip to Michigan after we'd selected the name involved more driving that usual. But with her new attitude, the time in cars was not nearly as difficult as it had been previously. Driving doesn't ruffle Bond girls, and no longer would it aggravate Nancy.

***

The nickname, however, did not stick. I could never bring myself to call her Jaguar; Nancy never used the name for herself. While neither of us ever used it as a proper name, we did start employing *jaguar* to designate an attitude and those who embody it. Much like the journalist Newfield found in the boxer Frazier a representative for the qualities he prized and wanted to develop in himself, Nancy and I came to think of the jaguar as our symbol of ideal characteristics.

Around the time I was developing an appreciation for jaguars, I was also reconsidering and writing about the punk-rock period of my high school years, and finding some parallels between the do-it-yourself dynamism of punk and jaguars' determination. "We got that attitude," the Bad Brains proclaim in a track from the 1983 album *Rock for Light*. "Hey we got the P.M.A.," or Positive Mental Attitude they explain in what must be one of the very few instances of hardcore song lyrics printed complete with explanatory footnote. "Attitude" also appeared a year before on a cassette-only, self-titled release that achieved something like legendary status subsequently. However, it was the *Rock for Light* version – not the one from the so-called Reachout International Records, or ROIR, tape – that I remembered. After my leather-jacket-and-combat-boots period of teenage rebellion, for which bands like the Bad Brains provided the soundtrack, I branched out and started listening to other sorts of music. Thus, for about a decade, I was unaware of another Bad Brains recording, dubbed *Black Dots*, which documents a session from 1979 but went unreleased until 1996. It also contained a version of the song. Appreciation of one style of music does not preclude sustained interest in or openness to others. The Bad Brains, who combined punk rock with reggae, demonstrate this, and I thought they'd be a good group to revisit decades later. I found that their work, particularly the multiple takes of "Attitude," still resonated with me.

The Bad Brains have the P.M.A.; Nancy and I have the jaguar attitude. A jaguar doesn't let the bastards get him down. A jaguar doesn't expect others to provide for him; he goes out and gets what he wants. A jaguar is relentless and strong-willed. Rather than dwelling on the ways people will inevitably disappoint you, the inevitability of plans not working out, the certainty that things will go wrong or the predictably unpleasant aspects of daily life (including certain modes of transportation), we opted for the jaguar outlook.

Whether labeled P.M.A. or the Frazier method, it's the sort of mindset the narrator of Albert Camus's *The Plague* displays. Confined to a town beset by a deadly epidemic, Dr. Bernard Rieux continues to administer to his patients. He does not give up and he does not give in. "If you refuse to be beaten," Rieux says, "you have some pleasant surprises." (The fictional physician's creator, who frequently declared that nothing was more absurd than to die in a car accident, died in a car accident.)

It's the sort of preparedness for difficulties and willingness to confront them that the title character of *Lawrence of Arabia* exhibits. In an early scene, one that foreshadows thematic elements explored throughout the film, someone asks how a person can extinguish a lighted match with his fingers without hurting himself. The trick, Peter O'Toole's T.E. Lawrence explains, is to not mind the pain. Pain and hardship, he suggests, cannot be avoided, but they can be faced and they can be handled. Individuals can train themselves to endure without complaining. (The film opens with the motorcycle accident that killed Lawrence.)

Trepidation about car travel may not be a monumental difficulty comparable with potentially deadly contagion and the oppressive regulations of quarantine (or occupation, if *The Plague* is read as an allegory of the Resistance) or an arduous trek across a fiery desert on camelback. That is not the point. A jaguar deals with whatever needs to be dealt with, and maintains its fierce P.M.A. at all times.

Our jaguar approach to challenges big and small has proven useful in ways beyond what first spurred its conceptualization. In addition to getting over a particular fear following a car crash, the jaguar perspective has proven helpful in getting into better physical condition (jaguars like to move) and in being more disciplined and productive with regard to our various creative pursuits (jaguars have a champion's work ethic), to provide just a couple examples of its application.

***

I am interested here in jaguars' representative potential, not coincidences. While the expensive cars that take their name from the animal do indeed figure in several of the Bond films, the vehicles are not what bind together the people mentioned above. The car services that ferry travelers to New York area airports usually maintain fleets of black Lincoln Town Cars or other similar American models. Our accident occurred in an Audi. Camus's last journey did not take place in a Jaguar (it was in a Facel-Vega). While the British car-maker traces its origins back to a company founded by motorcycle enthusiasts who first built sidecars, Lawrence's fatal ride was on one of his several bikes manufactured by George Brough. However, seeing jaguar-like characteristics in both Camus and Lawrence is not purely accidental. The author of *The Stranger* and *The Myth of Sisyphus* fondly invoked Lawrence's line about the aim of revolution, which, as Camus put in the Resistance newspaper *Combat*, is to "give human life a chance." Giving life a chance and struggling to improve it – that's what jaguars are all about.

***

In *Octopussy,* a Bond girl reveals a tattoo of an octopus, the symbol of the group to which she belongs. It's on her lower back.

Nancy and I both have jaguar tattoos. Mine leaps across my left arm; hers stands – composed, calm and confident – on her lower back.

WEIGHT LOSS: A LOVE STORY

"Don't worry about that; I'll tell you when to stop," the doctor replied when, after being told to lose weight, I asked how much.

Of course, I'd known I could have stood to shed a few pounds, twenty-five or so, I figured, based on nothing much. I had a vague idea that such a number seemed neither like a great deal of extra weight to be carrying around nor like an intimidatingly large amount to drop. I chose to overlook, then, how my physician's remark implied that I had a long road before me. Some minor adjustments, I thought, would take care of things. Besides, without a firm statement of what I ought to weigh, I didn't feel a great deal of pressure. After all, while saying he'd let me know when I arrived at the proper weight may have suggested it was a ways off, the doctor had also expressed surprise at what the scale read. "Where do you keep it," he'd joked.

Because of its suggestion of weakness and failure, fatness leads to jokes, which can, as better jokes do, offer penetratingly serious insights. When I was a thin teenager, a friend's father liked to rib corpulent acquaintances by saying: "I see you've been losing weight" – long pause – "over your belt." Beyond insulting a person's appearance, the crack implied an inability to rein in gluttonous impulses. The punch line withdraws the implied compliment over size of the joke's set up. In *One Fat Englishman,* Kingsley Amis inverts a cliché about fatness when he writes: "Outside every fat man there was an even fatter man trying to close in." The line points to the slob's passivity, as if getting bigger were something that just happened to people rather than something caused by their behavior. Clive James made a similar statement, though without the same comic intent, when he told the novelist's son, Martin Amis: "It's not that you *get* fat. One day your whole body just *turns into* fat." (The younger Amis relays the remark in *Experience*, a memoir in which he expresses concern over the size of his ass.) The jokes hint that obesity results from inattention.

Jokes can also deflect focus from seriousness. If my doctor could talk about my weight with light-hearted banter, it couldn't be that big of deal. Right?

That's how I treated it, like it wasn't much of a problem. After that check-up, I swore I wouldn't have potato chips at lunch time, or at least I'd munch on them less frequently. If I didn't take my light-style yogurt to the office in the morning, I'd buy one on the way instead of substituting a bagel with cream cheese as I had been wont to do. For a while I'd been thinking about getting a bicycle. With the help of a bike-enthusiast friend, my wife, Nancy, got me one as a birthday gift. I did get into the habit of riding it on weekends, if the weather was clear. Gradually I increased the number of laps I made around Prospect Park, which Frederick Law Olmsted and Calvert Vaux, who also planned Central Park, designed to include a 3.3-mile circular road that attracted Brooklyn bike riders. Over time I even lost my dread of the fairly steep hill that menaced me so greatly early on in my cycling days. A man on a unicycle passing me on that incline motivated me to work a little harder. Moving slower than the packs of riders in colorful tight-fitting costumes on sleek Italian racing bikes was one thing, but that was too much to accept.

I did manage to lose a few pounds. Nowhere near twenty-five, surely, but still, I was making progress, I told myself. When you're six feet and three inches tall and weigh 250 pounds, you can lose five or ten pounds without anyone, including yourself, registering any change in appearance. Still, even if I could not see or feel a difference, it helped to know I had moved in the right direction.

Because I'd never suffered any serious health problems, I'd had not given much thought to my physical condition. My awareness that I was overweight never felt like it required serious attention or immediate action. For a person who was desk-bound for much of every day, I was reasonably active, I told myself. Never one to go to a gym, I was not exactly a lay-about either. Nancy and I had always been great walkers, for instance. I never felt like my size impeded me or kept from doing what I wanted to do. I found it very easy to ignore my weight problem.

Then news came about my wife's health that caused me to rethink my lackadaisical attitude about my own. Unlike mine, her body constantly reminded her of its existence and demanded vigilance. In her case, weight was never a problem. Though she may have added a couple pounds over the first ten or so years of our marriage, she remained slender – a wisp of a thing as I called her. For someone so far from obese to receive a diagnosis of diabetes felt cruelly ironic, even perverse. Genetic inheritance can work exactly that way.

Having earlier been told she had hypoglycemia, Nancy had been fully aware of food's impact on her well-being. With the arrival of long-feared diabetes, however, came a need to be even more conscientious and systematic about consumption. Told she could manage her condition through her diet, she was determined to do so. She vowed to live a long, healthy life.

And so did I. How could I simultaneously support her efforts to preserve her health but disregard my own? Even if I did not have the disease, I could certainly take better care of myself. More importantly, I wanted to help her any way I could. One small thing I could do, I reckoned, was eat what she ate.

Her doctor had put her on what he called the "Black Panther Diet," which primarily involved avoiding "white" food such as sugar, flour and potatoes. With diabetes, counting carbohydrates became necessary. The goal was not to cut them out altogether – which would be incredibly difficult to do – but to restrict intake to a certain level, one appropriate for a body not producing enough insulin to handle unregulated quantities of glucose in its blood.

Eating the same way as her was the least I could do, but I wanted to do more than only that. Exercise is especially important for diabetics. Physical activity can aid in controlling blood sugar levels. With diabetes comes increased risk for cardiovascular disease, which makes strengthening the heart and circulatory system vital. While I did not have high blood pressure, it did run in my family, and while my cholesterol was not too high, it was getting close. Obviously, we both could stand to benefit from greater concentration on fitness.

I committed myself to attaining the correct size and shape for my body, and that meant exercise – real exercise. Weekend rides in the park were not enough. An apparatus turning a bicycle into a stationary machine (another gift from Nancy – our efforts to be healthy were mutually supportive) meant weather no longer affected the quality or frequency of my cycling. As an extra benefit, oblivious park patrons who fail to watch what they are doing as they cross the bike path with their baby carriages and dogs ceased to bother me. I added other activities – weights, a pull-up bar, sit ups and push ups and so on – to what became an almost daily routine. After work, we would exercise. On the weekends, we would exercise intensively after breakfast. Though I would do something on most days, I varied the sessions somewhat. At the very least, I would spend time on the bicycle. Some days I would pick up the dumbbells, other days I focused on the abdomen.

Practically against my will I developed an appreciation for what had seemed like a gratingly vapid slogan: Just do it. Though I never purchased shoes or apparel from the company that built ubiquitous advertising campaigns around the motto, I did come to understand the thinking behind it. I would not permit myself to say, "I don't feel like exercising today." I simply would – here I go – do it. Later on, I heard Ian MacKaye, the epitome of punk rock virtues, member of many bands and co-founder of fiercely independent Dischord Records, discuss how a Nike-sponsored event had appropriated for a flyer an image from the cover of an album by Minor Threat, one of his former groups. Some listeners seemed disappointed when the resolutely anti-corporate MacKaye said he chose not to pursue a potentially lengthy court fight, especially since the trivial incident did not really bother him all that much. He had other ways he wanted to spend his time and energy. Some in the audience laughed further along in his talk on creating art on one's own terms when he used the famous commandment himself. I didn't; I understood precisely how that could happen. Unless we had after-work plans that would have made exercise impractical, I would workout everyday without interruption. Although Nancy's doctor said that her body would function best if she kept it fit, it got to the point where I was working out more often than she was. I just did it.

It worked. For both of us. Boxing, a sport in which athletes must attend closely to their weight, had given me, strictly as a spectator, a perspective on size, one that I found changed as my body did. Previously I could not comprehend how tall fighters were able to campaign in divisions like middleweight (160 pounds), super middleweight (168) or even light heavyweight (175). When I was far from those weight classes I could not imagine being anything other than a heavyweight, for which there is no weight limit. At the beginning of the May when Nancy's diagnosis came down, I weighed 240 pounds; by the beginning of the following year I had reduced that by 70. I toned up some, but I never developed the muscular-but-still-slim physique of an in-shape fighter. That had not been my aim. I did gain a greater appreciation of the work that goes into one as well an understanding of it being a realizable state. Nancy also lost a couple pounds, but more importantly felt much healthier and in greater control of the state of her body.

Changing weight class did not change only my size. There were several unforeseen developments. Change followed change, and with me the alterations were not confined to my body.

I never wanted to put much time or energy into clothing: I hate shopping for it and I prefer not to think much about what I am going to put on each morning. It would not be honest to say I didn't care at all about my appearance. Anyone claiming to be vanity-free is a liar, probably one quite proud of his or her carefully cultivated above-it-all self-image. We express our vanity in different ways. I have never understood overweight people who wore clothing that accentuated their least attractive features: tight waistbands squeezing rolls of fatty flesh, short shirts showing off mushy guts and other similarly ill-advised, bulge-making, flab-showing choices. I may not have been able to make myself look thin, but I did not dress as though I were and hope others played along with a delusion. Aware that I was soft in the middle, I did not want to draw attention to my stomach. I did not try to disguise it either. I never thought leaving my shirt untucked made me look slimmer, but comfort was a consideration as well. Loose fitting clothes do tend to suit fat folks best. In order to streamline the dressing process, all my black or dark blue trousers could be effortlessly paired with any of my solid, generally dark shirts.

When none of your clothes fit anymore, you lose the luxury of not thinking about your wardrobe. I reached the point when I had lost twenty-five pounds and realized I still had more losing to do. I did not need to be told that I had not yet reached the stopping point. This forced me to accept, grudgingly, that I would need to buy new clothes, but ones to cover my shrinking self only during a transitional period. What I owned no longer fit, but I knew I was going to get smaller. Perhaps people for whom fashion dictates the wearing of certain things for a single "season" before moving on to the latest style are accustomed to regarding clothing as disposable, but I expected what I wore to be with me for years. (I never could convince Nancy that socks with holes did not need to be thrown away because shoes would cover them. I got used to hearing "Really, you're keeping those?" as we folded laundry.) Buying new clothes was no longer a matter of replacing items that had reached, or gone slightly beyond, the point of being worn out. However, my habitual mode of dressing so as *not* to draw attention to myself necessitated getting apparel that actually fit to replace the too-large clothes drooping over me. As I moved along the road to the right weight, my clothes crossed from slightly baggy to hobo shabby. Wearing shirts that look like they belong to a bigger man with trousers that bunch together in places when your belt is cinched tight enough to hold them up just leads to impertinent questions.

What surprised me most as I developed healthier habits and grew increasingly fit was how many people would ask if I was sick. Presumably unaccustomed to people effectively ridding themselves of unwanted pounds, acquaintances seemed more prone to assume I had some sort of wasting disease. Many people, after remarking on my having lost weight, would proceed to ask whether I had done so on purpose. Having read so often that the majority of Americans were overweight, with a significant percentage qualifying as obese, I wondered where these people were who were losing weight by accident. Some inquisitors may have been trying to be kind and considerate. After all, I had started shrinking rapidly. Others may have resented the change. I became convinced that, just as there are alcoholics aggravated rather than pleased by the loss of a drinking buddy to sobriety, there are non-boxing heavyweights who are jealous of and annoyed by those who successfully depart the ranks of the overweight and obese. Whatever prompted queries regarding my condition, and whether alterations in it were deliberate, one thing a person putting a great deal of effort into improving his health does not want to hear is that he looks ill. I knew that swimming in oversize clothes did not help the situation.

So I broke down and bought clothing I knew would only cover me for weeks or months before replacements became necessary. I was glad when I arrived at a point where I could finally get dark trousers and solid, generally dark shirts that could be mixed and matched for years to come.

While my mode of dress did not completely change, I confess that I did start to pay a bit more attention to my appearance. I no longer left shirttails hanging out. I started wearing clothes that actually fit properly. If I still saw no reason to attract attention to my appearance, I did not need to deflect it entirely either.

More important than matters sartorial, I think, was how I came to think about food. More specifically, I actually did start to think about food rather than just indiscriminately shoveling it in. Weighing less and, thus, eating less food meant becoming significantly more involved with what I ate than I had been before. Nancy continued to do most of the cooking. She had always enjoyed doing it, and restrictions on certain ingredients created new culinary challenges, to put the matter positively. I always helped with the shopping, but now my assistance extended beyond merely helping carry and put away groceries. I started to do more in the kitchen than just the dishes. I still followed her lead but I also learned more about ingredients and their combination as well as techniques for meal-making that I had not been aware of previously. I started trying to help come up with ideas for meals rather than leaving all the planning to her and in doing so came to appreciate just how much deliberation the art of cooking really involves.

Part of my late-forming willingness to pay attention to food concerned not just preparation but also portions. Deciding not to be fat means refraining from care-free indulgence. It means restraining consumption to reasonable quantities. Knowing the carbohydrate content and other nutritional properties of a dish requires a sense of appropriate serving sizes. We became scrupulous label readers and carb calculators. We bought, and used, a kitchen scale.

I became convinced that the reason so many people fail when they go on weight-loss diets is because they do not bother to learn about what they eat. With no understanding of the nutritional properties of what they consume as they try this or that gimmick, they never develop an understanding of food. Reliance on special pre-packaged fare, as some diets demand, cannot substitute for knowing how to select food intelligently on one's own. Strict avoidance of certain types of food or exclusive focus on others cannot replace recognizing what you need and what you don't, what foods meet those needs and which don't, and acting accordingly.

In addition to questions about my health, I often had to field variations on "What's you're secret?" There is no secret. Eat less, but also eat the right things. Move. I never allowed myself to answer the question so bluntly – I did not want to exchange my former slovenly sloth for insufferable smugness – but I always wanted to say: "There are no shortcuts." There really aren't any, after all, even if there's no consoling, soothing way to convey this to those who most need to accept it. For years, I had been such a person – a person losing weight over his belt. Despite what Clive James said to his friend Martin Amis, fat does not just happen, unless expanders look away from the state of their bodies. I started regarding my once larger physique as evidence of too little introspection. The fatter man could only have closed in on me because I ignored his approach – and his arrival.

In working on body weight, an obsessive type can simultaneously end up struggling against a tendency to swing the pendulum too far the other way. (Boxers struggling to make a specific class's designated weight frequently develop eating disorders, for instance.) I am aware that frequent questions about my health meant some people thought I looked like I had lost too much weight or had done so too quickly. I recall a former professor of mine – a gaunt, reed-like, even sickly-looking man – who revealed that he once had been hugely overweight and that even though he knew intellectually that that was no longer the case, he still sometimes thought of himself that way. At times, I remind myself that I do not have to deny myself constantly, and probably should not. Eating to lose and eating to maintain are not the same. I can comprehend my old teacher's mode of self-perception, but, fortunately, I do not share it. I do continue to pay close attention to what I consume, and I insist on self-discipline, but I rarely step on a scale, and I permit myself sensible amounts of treats, like Nancy's sugar-free, whole wheat-flour baked goods.

When, not long after I achieved a healthy weight, I was told that I had an inguinal hernia in need of surgery and that while recovering I should refrain from exercise and any strenuous activity, I did not dwell on risks related to being cut open. I did not give much thought to the dangers of anesthesia. Instead, I feared how the six-week interruption in my workout regimen would affect my weight. (The doctor who first informed me I would probably have to have an operation was not the same one who told me start losing weight. By the time I had followed that jokester's advice I had switched primary care physicians.)

I didn't enjoy that relatively immobile time, but it turned out to be reassuring. I did not regain lost pounds during my stretch of enforced inactivity. I did not revert to my erstwhile unthinking indulgence of appetites. Indeed, I adjusted my intake to suit my temporarily sedentary state. After the designated layoff, I returned to regular exercise. Not facing imminent danger of ballooning to my former size, I even allowed myself a regular day off from my workout routine.

Perhaps an expanded awareness of the extent of one's control over his or her body, an increased (but hardly excessive) attention to appearance, and a greater interest in physical fitness and nutrition are all completely predictable consequences of substantial weight loss. Perhaps slimming down would not have been possible with out concomitant alterations in outlook and attitude. Perhaps I should have realized that changing one aspect of my existence would affect others.

But those were not the only changes.

Immediately before and after my surgery, I spent plenty of time in doctors' waiting rooms. Anyone who says he or she does not mind doing that must be as dishonest as a person claiming to be without vanity. ("I wait, I wait, I wait,"

MacKaye sings in a Fugazi song. "My time is like water down a drain.") However, one scene from that otherwise wasted time remains with me. There was nothing unusual about the elderly couple I observed sitting across the room from me. What could be more ordinary than seeing aged individuals at a medical clinic? I probably only noticed them because when it was time for the pair to depart, the women moved so very slowly. Her husband helped her across the room and then went to bring the car around to a spot near the building's entrance. Sometimes the sight of advanced deterioration can seem unrelentingly sad. But that was not what I took away from seeing this couple. My decision to improve my health in tandem with my wife's intensified care for hers resulted in my coming to share some of her interests and becoming more involved in activities she enjoys. The kitchen stopped seeming like the site of chores. I became convinced that (just) doing it – and doing it together – helped make regular exercise a real habit. What could be more intimate than participating in the maintenance of each other's health? What does caring for each other mean if not that? I am not eager for us to be exactly like that couple – I want plenty more active years ahead of us – but I know that forfeiting more time to waiting rooms is inevitable. When we reach that age when care shifts from improving or maintaining health to managing and easing its inevitable decline, being together to accompany and assist one another in unpleasant places, like that elderly man and woman I noticed were, can be dismissed as nothing special only if love can be as well. I never expected to find something to admire while sitting and waiting, waiting, waiting.

At Corinth two temples stood side by side, the temple of Violence and the temple of Necessity.

– Albert Camus, "The Minotaur" (1939)

PART V

FIGHTERS & WRITERS

FIGHTERS & WRITERS

A banner hanging on a wall at Gleason's Gym testifies to boxing's enduring appeal for writers. The Brooklyn boxing institution takes its motto – "Now, whoever has courage and a strong and collected spirit in his breast let him come forward, lace on the gloves and put up his hands" – from Virgil. From antiquity to the present, writers have been fascinated by humans fighting, seeing in the sport something akin to their own efforts. Appropriately, two contending views of the sport emerged. In the red corner stand those who see meetings between nearly naked and practically unprotected combatants as simple and straightforward pursuits of victory through the unmediated imposition of their wills. Writers like to see them as symbolic of their own lonely quests after the elusive truth. In the blue corner are those who see fights as far more complex endeavors fraught with meaning and metaphorical possibilities. Rather than immediately comprehensible physical contests, fights are primarily mental challenges. Far from being basic and true, boxing involves trickery and deception. In one camp, boxing is free of artifice; in the other, it is full of it.

José Torres, a boxer turned writer, takes the latter view. The former world light heavyweight champion relishes describing boxing as a game of intelligence, cunning, deception and confidence. Some of his favorite boxing stories involve Muhammad Ali, a boxer with special appeal for writers. After he retired from the ring, Torres became one of the many authors (such as Murray Kempton, Norman Mailer,

George Plimpton, Ishmael Reed, Wole Soyinka, Gay Talese, Hunter S. Thompson and Tom Wolfe) to write about Ali. Long after committing them to print, Torres continued to tell his Ali stories very much like he did in *Sting Like a Bee*, which he co-authored with sportswriter Bert Sugar.

The first time I met Torres he was with Paul Johnson, a former club fighter who later became chairman of the Boxers Organizing Committee, a group set up to form a union for professional boxers. Johnson set the stage for his friend to tell some of his favorite stories by recounting a time when the two were speaking together at a university. Paul had been telling students about what he then thought of as the fundamental honesty at the heart of boxing. Torres interrupted him.

"Boxers are liars," he said.

Torres believes that boxing is "not really a contest of physical ability." He elaborated his ideas in a subsequent meeting: "I felt it was a contest always of character and intelligence. And I always felt what made a champion and an ordinary fighter was that, the character, the will to win, more than the physicality. Because when you are up there, among the best, the physicality is the same." Torres takes evident pleasure in explaining why Ali was *not* the greatest boxer, but was a genius in the ring. Doing so affords him the opportunity to recall fond memories of Ali and legendary trainer Cus D'Amato while also illustrating his point about boxers being liars. In his book on Ali, he starts the story with D'Amato, the guide to three world champions: Floyd Patterson, Torres himself and Mike Tyson. "[Ali] is not a good fighter, so says D'Amato, much less a great fighter. But he is champion of the world. Which, believing Cus, and I do, makes Ali a genius...." He continues, in virtually the same words he spoke to me decades after the 1971 book appeared:

> Ali is not a great fighter in the conventional sense
> that Sugar Ray Robinson, Willie Pep and Joe Louis
> were. Each of these fighters knew every punch and

every move and added some tricks to the book, that unwritten book whose teachings are passed on from gym to gym and are the nearest thing we have to our own culture.... We have a man who does not have the physical greatness of the greatest men of other times, yet no professional has been able to beat him.... The explanation is simple. Muhammad Ali is a genius.... Don't watch Ali's gloves, arms or legs when he's fighting. Watch his brains.

Other writers have made similar claims in connection with other fighters. Jack Dempsey's "overwhelming power made many people overlook the calculation that went into every punch he threw," Roger Kahn writes in *A Flame of Pure Fire.* "In that regard, he was a thinking, even intellectual boxer." In the first volume of *A Man Without Qualities,* published not long after Dempsey's reign as heavyweight champion ended, novelist Robert Musil prefigured Torres and D'Amato with observations like this one: "the tricks and dodges used by an inventive mind in going through the logical operations of a mathematical problem are really not very different from the ring-craft displayed by a well-trained body." A.J. Liebling, who composed numerous entertainingly digressive, erudite articles on boxing for *The New Yorker* in the 1950s and early 1960s, distinguishes between "the *ruffian* approach" and that of "the *reasoner* inside the ring."

Part of boxers' "culture," in the view of Torres and his fellow thinkers, is the ability to lie successfully. As Jeremy Campbell notes in his so-called history of falseness, *A Liar's Tale,* "when winning is the important factor, deceitfulness is a kind of ethic...." From a technical standpoint, Ali did plenty "wrong" but excelled nonetheless because of his cleverness, his ability to con his opponents. He perfected the liar's ethic.

Of course, eventually Ali did meet opponents who could beat him, but even then his genius was evident. *Sting Like a Bee* ends with Ali's first bout with Joe Frazier, which Ali lost. Frazier's trainer, Eddie Futch, told Ali's biographer, Thomas

Hauser, that Ali still successfully tricked his fighter during the bout: "Joe should have knocked him out in the eleventh round, but Ali conned him out of it. We teased Joe about that later, because he didn't realize at the time that he was being conned. Ali was in trouble. He got hit with a left hook, and was hurt very badly, and he exaggerated the fact that he was hurt like he was clowning. He gave Joe exaggerated moves, and Joe walked casually to Ali all the way across the ring. We call that 'The Long March.' It gave Ali extra time and kept Joe from scoring a knockout. By exaggerating, Ali made Joe think that he was fooling. He conned him good."

Ali did eventually regain the championship, and he did so by again digging into his bag of tricks. He prevailed over George Foreman by fighting a very different fight than most expected. Rather than dancing around the ring, using his speed to outmaneuver the famously hard-hitting Foremen, Ali positioned himself on the ropes, allowing Forman to tire himself out throwing punches. While the "rope-a-dope" might not have been a good practice if long-term health had been a primary concern, it was a successful tactic that morning in Zaire. Looking back on the "Rumble in the Jungle," Foreman conceded that Ali had him fooled.

The sport, as Ali so skillfully showed, shares elements with confidence games. In *The Big Con: The Story of the Confidence Man*, David Mauer observes that such deceptions are not as simple as unscrupulous exploitation of the naïve. Con men prey not on the gullible and good but on the devious. A mark must have more than money ready for the taking. As Mauer puts it, "he must also have what grifters term 'larceny in his veins' – in other words, he must want something for nothing, or be willing to participate in an unscrupulous deal." The delicious irony of this is that con men are themselves susceptible to swindles. They have the very trait, the "thieves' blood," that they try to exploit in others.

Confidence games would not be so compelling if they were as simple as taking candy from a baby. Cons, whether big or small, take some ingenuity; otherwise they would be mere thievery. Con men and their targets navigate a world in which not everyone is honest and not everything is as it appears. Thus, confidence games have provided artists such as Herman Melville and David Mamet with material because they entail questions of practical epistemology: Who can you trust? How do you know your information is reliable? And how can you use it to your advantage?

The same is true with boxing at its best, at least according to one way of looking at it. Boxing is much more than two brutes beating up on each other. It is also more complicated than one fighter tricking an unprepared dupe: mismatches may be a part of the game, but they are boring. When the fighters are well matched physically and also shrewd strategists, with each seeking to exploit the other's desire to find an opening, an advantage, a weakness – then the sport rises to the level of art.

An art with very real consequences. As Mauer observes, a confidence man "cannot fool his associates for long. Either he takes off the scores or he doesn't, and he stands or falls in his profession by the record he makes for himself." The importance of cunning in boxing doesn't lessen the very real physical perils. Boxing is not professional wrestling; the violence is real. The sport's mental aspect, which Torres so prizes, comes into play when physical abilities are comparable. Ali, the "Louisville Lip," was able to back up his bluster, even if he did so with an unorthodox style.

The idea that boxers, individuals who choose to engage in a brain-damaging game, are smart might strike the uninitiated as peculiar if not ridiculous. Indeed, the strangeness of associating fighters with intelligence caused some to doubt that Torres actually wrote his books (he also published a biography of Tyson). A rumor suggested that Mailer actually wrote Torres's portions of the Ali book. Jonathan Rendell, in his brilliantly titled *This Bloody Mary Is the Last Thing I Own*, recounts hearing a version of it. "Mailer wrote it for him," the man on the next barstool explained to Rendell. "That was the deal they had. Torres taught Mailer how to box and Mailer wrote *Sting Like a Bee* for him. Ain't that something?" Mailer and Torres were friends, and Mailer admitted to providing editorial aid to the fighter, who did give the novelist some boxing pointers. Still, Mailer insists that the book is genuine and not another instance of a boxer's con game. For he did share his friend's views about pugilistic trickery. In his 1975 account of the Ali-Foreman fight, Mailer explicitly invokes the D'Amato-Torres philosophy, a key component of which is that skilled boxers can block or evade any punch they can see coming. "Champions were great liars," Mailer explains in *The Fight*. "They had to be. Once you knew what they thought, you could hit them. So their personalities became masterpieces of concealment."

Norman Mailer & Muhammad Ali, 1965

However, Mailer elsewhere expresses the other widely held view of boxing, the one in which fighters are heroic warriors, which is precisely how Mailer imagined writers, or at least himself. Although the solitary writer slouching at a desk seems worlds apart from a well-conditioned fighter confronting an opponent in a ring, Mailer saw them as very similar. In *The Spooky Art,* he insists the demands writing makes on a novelist, including physical ones, are much like those a fighter confronts:

> Only a writer can know how much damage writing a novel can do to you. It's an unnatural activity to sit at a desk and squeeze words out of yourself. Various kinds of poisons – essences of fatigue – get secreted through your system. As you age it grows worse. I believe that is one of the reasons I've been so interested in prizefighters. I think often of the aging boxer who has to get into shape for one more fight and knows the punishment it will wreak on his body.... Even if he wins the fight – even if he wins it well – he is not going to get a new purchase on life out of a dazzling success, not in the way he did as a young fighter. That's also true of my profession. Often, you have to make grave decisions: Am I going to attempt this difficult venture or not?

Put another way, writing is hard, just as boxing, more obviously, is hard. In this comparison of fighters and writers, Mailer does not invoke cunning and craftiness. Instead, he stresses earnest exertion.

Mailer goes even further in his search for commonality, arguing that boxers and writers are similar not only in the rigors they put themselves through but also in their willingness to hurt others:

> Just as a fighter has to feel that he possesses the right to do physical damage to another man, so a writer has to be ready to take chances with his readers' lives. If you're trying for something at all

> interesting or difficult, then you cannot predict what the results of your work will be. If it's close enough to the root, people can be physically injured reading you. Full of heart, he was also heartless – a splendid oxymoron. That can be the epitaph for many a good novelist.

Mailer's "splendid oxymoron" clearly applies to many a good boxer. However, he almost certainly exaggerates both the challenges a novelist faces and the effect he or she can have on a reader. Yet he clearly liked the idea of having a fighter's heartless heart – his will, determination, drive and competitiveness – beating in his chest. For him, boxing serves as a handy metaphor for what he imagined was his risky, intensely masculine style of writing.

Like Mailer, another friend of Torres also gave expression to both conceptions of the sport without achieving a synthesis of them. When the boxing-as-trickery notion was useful, journalist Jack Newfield used it. When he wanted to point to a model of certain virtues, boxing again offered handy examples. Newfield believed the deceitful personalities involved in boxing provide a reason for writers' unflagging interest in the sport. "As in the record business and horse racing, almost everyone in boxing seems like a character," he writes in *Only in America: The Life and Crimes of Don King*. "That's why writers and filmmakers are drawn to it. Almost everyone in boxing is a colorful story teller with a touch of lunacy or larceny." It is certainly true that he chose to focus on one of boxing's colorful characters in King. A former numbers runner who killed two men, King became fabulously wealthy by using the rhetoric of racial solidarity to sign black boxers to his promotional company and then exploit them mercilessly, according to Newfield's account. Newfield finds conniving and cunning not only on the business side of the sport, but in the fights themselves. He discusses the Ali-Foreman bout in terms very similar to Mailer's, writing: "Boxing is based on deceit. Fighters are taught to lie – to conceal fatigue, mask pain, disguise intent with a feint, deny an injury, look one way and punch another." As the fights with Frazier and Foreman illustrate, the trickery extends beyond concealing intentions in order to avoid being hit; for Ali, it also meant baffling expectations.

Newfield changes tack when relating his own work to that of boxers, who then become paragons. For instance, in *Somebody's Gotta Tell It*, the story of his life as a newspaperman, Newfield, following Mailer's example, finds fighters worth emulating, but at the keyboard rather than the gym. Boxers' bravery and relentlessness ought to characterize a dogged journalist as well. He promotes what he calls the "Joe Frazier method" of journalism: "keep coming forward. Don't get discouraged. Be relentless. Don't stop moving your hands. Break the others guy's will."

One of Newfield's intellectual heroes writes about boxing as though it reflects the process of finding or creating meaning in an absurd world. Albert Camus describes boxers as "gods with cauliflower ears," giving some indication of the respect he has for athletes who, like Sisyphus, persevere through ultimately pointless endeavors. He also transmutes physical combat into the equivalent of a matter of language, viewing a fight as though it were an argument. Fighters' representative capabilities – their amply documented tendency to be regarded by spectators as the embodiment of a race, an ethnicity or a nationality – offer writers plenty of material to work with beyond mere athleticism. Camus explains how, for those in attendance at a fight he witnessed in Algeria between Amar from Oran and Pérez from Algiers, the boxers became stand-ins for their respective cities and how their bout became an extension of an ongoing rivalry between the two places. "Thus a page of history is unfolding in the ring. And the tough Oranese, backed by a thousand yelling voices, is defending against Pérez a way of life and the pride of a province." Spectators' responses to fighters' struggles often have more to do with such allegiances than with what the contestants actually do in the ring, and in describing boxers' moves Camus finds a parallel with disputation. "Truth forces me to admit that Amar is not conducting his discussion well. His argument has a flaw: he lacks reach. The slugger from Algiers, on the contrary, has the required reach in his argument. It lands persuasively between his contradictor's eyes." What writer wouldn't want to have such a reach?

Joyce Carol Oates, for one, expresses impatience with the sort of "hellish-writerly metaphor" in which boxing serves to stand for something else. She concedes that skill, courage and intelligence can all be observed in a boxing match. She even "can entertain the proposition that life is a metaphor for boxing." However, boxing itself is, quite simply, "the most primitive and terrifying of contests." Her *On Boxing* does not offer extravagant assertions of fighters as avatars of artistry or as unrecognized geniuses. She briefly surveys other writers' writing on boxing and is impressed by little of it. She dislikes Liebling and does not think Ernest Hemingway's boxing stories rank among his best. She admires aspects of Mailer's work on the subject, but concludes that in the end he gets it wrong. "It seems clear to this reader at least that Mailer cannot establish a connection between himself and the boxers: he tries heroically but he cannot understand them," she writes. Whereas Camus likens boxing to an argument, Oates stresses its wordlessness, its lack of language. Whereas he sees fighters carrying on historical disputes, she counters that men fighting and those watching them belong "to no historical time." For Oates, boxing is not like something else. It is certainly not like writing, as it was for Mailer, Newfield and others. Instead, "boxing is only like boxing." If she finds truth in boxing, it is of a much more diminished and melancholy sort.

Rendell fell into the Johnson camp, the camp that sought truth in the sport, only to conclude that viewing boxing as expressive of some deep meaning can only lead to disappointment. In *This Bloody Mary,* his memoir of experiences in the boxing world, he recalls being a teenager looking at the photos in *Ring* magazine of ritualistic post-fight events – the announcement of the decision and the victor consoling the vanquished – and thinking: "It was as if all of them, the winners and losers and the managers and trainers, had touched something that only they could know about, something big, like truth." Later, when the romance was gone and he'd seen enough of the fight game, he concludes that its connection to the truth was very different than he'd initially thought. "Boxing had been leading me to a truth after all, but only to the truth about boxing. And the truth was just a story itself, the first addictive dance under the chandeliers, and then the doomed roller coaster ride on thousands of blue curves." The sort of truth he discovers is fighters dying in their twenties or living but with irreparable damage. For him, too, Ali becomes symbolic of boxing's truth. Rendell describes meeting the former champion, who required an hour to eat a bowl of soup. The fighter once famous for his quickness and prowess now had to move carefully, deliberately and slowly in order not to dribble.

The competing views of boxing – the notion that it is an honest expression of man's nature versus the belief that it entails artful deception as well as the more obvious physical challenges – also appear in W.C. Heinz's 1958 novel *The Professional.* Doc Carroll, a boxing manager, holds both, without acknowledging the paradox of viewing boxing as essentially truthful and involving much trickery. Explaining why he likes boxing, Doc says he sees the "truth of life" in it, and that truth includes "that remnant of the animal in man." He says, "I find man revealing himself more completely in fighting than in any other form of expressive endeavor. It's the war all over again, and they license it and sell tickets to it and people go to see it because, without even realizing it, they see this truth in it." Later he tells his fighter, Eddie: "There's only so many punches. Everybody knows what they are. You've got to con the other guy into walking into them. It's thinking, first of all." If Doc's theories of boxing can be reconciled at all, it is by concluding that the essential truth, as revealed by boxing, is that man is a thinking beast, violent and clever, basic in animal desires and inclined toward misdirection to satisfy them. Doc favors the fundamental-honesty-of-boxing school, regarding cons as tactical rather then essential elements of the game. Eddie, who admits to Doc that he had not realized the role of trickery despite his nine years in boxing, loses the fight at the end of the book.

Another novelist, Darin Strauss, combines elements of history and fiction while mining the deep vein of literary possibilities offered by the idea of an intimate bond between pugilists and tricksters. If in Heinz's world deception is merely a part of boxing strategy, in Strauss's it throbs in the very heart of the sport. He very loosely based his 2002 novel *The Real McCoy* on the life of Norman Selby (a.k.a. Charles "Kid" McCoy), a crafty boxer who used his skills as a con man both in and out of the ring. Strauss remains faithful to these essential features even if he rearranges some facts to suit his story. ("We can change the normal way of things to fit our case," McCoy persuades one of the women he marries.) Like the historical McCoy, the fictionalized Kid was born in Indiana in the late nineteenth century, becomes known for his trademark "corkscrew punch," and has a colorful career as a charlatan. Strauss departs from the documented record of Selby's life in various ways. For instance, his "Virgil Selby" assumes the identity of another boxer known as Kid McCoy rather than creating the identity himself. The "real" McCoy won the vacant middleweight title in 1898, whereas Strauss has his McCoy win the welterweight title on January 1, 1900, by tricking the reigning champion into fighting what he thought was a mere exhibition. Strauss not only puts his

McCoy in a lower weight division, he stresses his character's slight build in order to highlight his mendacity in the ring.

Some of the fictional McCoy's comments about boxing make him sound like he could have come straight out of D'Amato's school of boxing philosophy. "I lack in bulk, but I make up for it in guile," McCoy explains in response to a reporter's commentary on his skin-and-bones physique. "Boys, artifice is a dignified defense." After successfully deploying his skin-ripping corkscrew punch in his title bout, McCoy is confronted by the deposed champ's wife: "Admit it, Mr. McCoy.... You lied to my husband to get the crown.... Admit your trickery!" "I don't admit it," he replies, "I *relish* in it." Of course, Strauss recognizes that boxing requires physical ability and is more than just deception. "McCoy knocked out Tommy Ryan thanks to real skill and the flimflam."

The contending views of boxing as either the brutal violence it immediately appears to be or something akin to art and equally complicated and ultimately irreducible to any simple explanation will not be settled for as long as human beings stage combat for enjoyment's sake. Given that boxing's roots can be traced back hundreds of years before Virgil and that writers continue to find something of themselves in fighters long after the sport's heyday in the twentieth century, imminent resolution seems unlikely. That does not mean the match ends in a draw, however. The conclusion of Paul Johnson and José Torres's well rehearsed account of their college speaking engagement has the union organizer wondering if he never became a better fighter than he did because he was too honest. It may be that writers and other successful practitioners of artifice (such as Ali) do not suffer from such scrupulousness. An indication of which perspective appears to have the upper hand might be found at Gleason's, a deliberately spare gym in a once-gritty neighborhood that later transformed itself into one filled with galleries, boutiques

and pricy loft apartments. Almost every time I have visited
the place to talk with its proprietor, Bruce Silverglade, there
have been camera crews filming movies or commercials or
taking photographs of models. Athletes still train there, but
meaning-making and spectacle-creation simultaneously occur
amid the sparring and shadow boxing. Artifice, whether
dignified or not, should never be underestimated.

SOURCES

Given its subject, *Fighters & Writers* discusses, describes, reviews and reacts to numerous other books, essays and articles. While my thinking about boxing and literature surely bears the traces of many other influences, I list below the works explicitly mentioned or made use of in these essays. Where applicable and possible, I also note when conversations or interviews factored into what I wrote.

Introduction
In the process of providing an overview of *Fighters & Writers* I refer to several works on boxing and related matters, some of which are not directly referred to in any other pieces.

Amis, Martin. 2001. *The War against Cliché: Essays and Reviews 1971 – 2000* (New York: Vintage International).

—. 1984. *Money: A Suicide Note* (New York: Penguin Books).

—. 1986. *The Moronic Inferno: And Other Visits to America* (London: Penguin Books).Hauser, Thomas. 1991. *Muhammad Ali: His Life and Times* (New York: Touchstone).

LeDuff, Charlie. 2004. *Work and Other Sins: Life in New York City and Thereabouts* (New York: Penguin Books).

Liebling, A.J. 1986. *Between Meals: An Appetite for Paris* (New York: North Point Press).

—. *The Earl of Louisiana* (Baton Rouge: Louisiana State University Press).

—. 1964. *Mollie & Other War Pieces* (New York: Schocken Books).

Manso, Peter. 2008. *Mailer: His Life and Times* (New York: Washington Square Press).

McIlvanney, Hugh. 2001. *The Hardest Game: McIlvanney on Boxing* (Chicago: Contemporary Books.

Mead, Chris. 1986. *Champion: Joe Louis: Black Hero in White America* (London: Robson Books).

Meyers, Jeffrey. 2000. *Orwell: Wintry Conscience of a Generation* (New York and London: W.W. Norton & Company).

Oates, Joyce Carol. 2002. *On Boxing*, expanded edition (New York: Ecco).

Plimpton, George. 2003. *Shadow Box: An Amateur in the Ring* (Guilford, Connecticut: The Lyons Press).

Rotella, Carlo. 2003. *Cut Time: An Education at the Fight* (Boston: Houghton Mifflin Company).

Sammons, Jeffery T. 1990. *Beyond the Ring: The Role of Boxing in American Society* (Urbana and Chicago: University of Illinois Press).

Ward, Geoffrey C. 2004. *Unforgivable Blackness: The Rise and Fall of Jack Johnson* (New York: Alfred A. Knopf).

The Ali Act

"The Ali Act," a review essay originally written for *Open Letters Monthly* (June 2008), examines several of the numerous books about Muhammad Ali, the fighter and the phenomenon. The quotation from Teddy Atlas in the essay comes from an interview I conducted with him in 2002.

Arkush, Michael. 2008. *The Fight of the Century: Ali vs. Frazier March 8, 1971* (Hoboken, NJ: John Wiley & Sons, Inc.)

Hauser, Thomas. 2005. *The Lost Legacy of Muhammad Ali* (Toronto: Sport Classic Books).

—. 1991. *Muhammad Ali: His Life and Times* (New York: Touchstone).

Kram, Mark. 2001. *Ghosts of Manila: The Fateful Blood Feud between Muhammad Ali and Joe Frazier* (New York: Perennial).

Liebling, A.J. 1990. *A Neutral Corner* (San Francisco: North Point Press).

Mailer, Norman. 1975. *The Fight* (New York: Vintage International).

Marqusee, Mike. 1999. *Redemption Song: Muhammad Ali and the Spirit of the Sixties* (London: Verso).

Oates, Joyce Carol. 2002. *On Boxing*, expanded edition (New York: Ecco).

Remnick, David. 1998. *King of the World: Muhammad Ali and the Rise of an American Hero* (New York: Random House).

Torres, José, and Bert Randolph Sugar. 1971. *Sting Like a Bee: The Muhammad Ali Story* (Chicago: Contemporary Books).

Seeing Stars

Cyril Connolly reflects on that fatal word *promise* and its association with the destruction of those thought to have had it in both his 1936 novel *The Rock Pool* and his 1938 memoir *Enemies of Promise*. The line quoted in "Seeing Stars" appears in both books, an instance of authorial recycling that would have fit in "Write, Repeat." "Seeing Stars," which was written for *The American Interest* (January/February 2010 as "Heels and Heroes"), also makes some use of the following works:

BOOKS DISCUSSED

Dunn, Katherine. 2009. *One Ring Circus: Dispatches from the World of Boxing* (Tucson, Arizona: Schaffner Press).

Early, Gerald (ed.). 1998. *The Muhammad Ali Reader* (New York: Rob Weisbach Books).

Liebling, A.J. 1990. *A Neutral Corner* (San Francisco: North
  Point Press).
Torres, José. 1989. *Fire & Fear: The Inside Story of Mike Tyson*
  (New York: Warner Books).
Tosches, Nick. 2000. *The Devil and Sonny Liston* (Boston:
  Little, Brown and Company).

FILMS DISCUSSED

Facing Ali, directed by Pete McCormack (2009)
Tyson, directed by James Toback (2009)
When We Were Kings, directed by Leon Gast (1996)

The Cinderella Man Fairytale
The book covered in this review arrived in bookstores around
the same time the similarly titled film starring Russell Crowe
as Jim Braddock showed in theaters. *FightNews* (17 May 2005)
used the title "Cinderella Man: The Book" to make perfectly
clear which work was being assessed, namely:

Schaap, Jeremy. 2005. *Cinderella Man: James J. Braddock, Max
  Baer, and the Greatest Upset in Boxing History* (Boston:
  Houghton Mifflin Company).

Health & Safety
Formerly an editor with the International Labor Office, I
contributed to the study of work-related risks and hazards
discussed in this essay (which first appeared on the *Ringside
and Training Principles* website in December 2005), but I did
not write the small piece on boxing. In the essay, I also
mention *Ringside and Training Principles,* a handbook edited by
Margaret Goodman and Flip Homansky and issued by the
Nevada State Athletic Commission for professional boxers
fighting in the state.

Stellman, Jeanne Mager (ed.). *Encyclopaedia of Occupational Health and Safety*, fourth edition (Geneva: International Labor Office).

There Are No Easy Answers

FightNews published a shorter version of this article the day after the *Wall Street Journal* article it discusses. A version of it subsequently appeared in an event program for a fight in November 2005. I interviewed the doctors mentioned in the piece, Flip Homansky and Margaret Goodman, on April 20, 2002, before a fight in Las Vegas.

A First-Class Sport

I interviewed John McCain in Washington DC on July 24, 2002, and New York City Police Commissioner Ray Kelly his office on April 16, 2002. I have also interviewed several others whose views I discuss, including Teddy Atlas, Thomas Hauser and Larry Holmes, but in this essay I rely on their books listed below. The essay also emerged from conversations held with the owner of Gleason's Gym and with fighters and trainers there. *Open Letters Monthly* published "A First-Class Sport" in August 2009.

Atlas, Teddy and Peter Alson. 2006. *Atlas: From the Streets to the Ring: A Son's Struggle to Become a Man.* (New York: Ecco).

Dunn, Katherine. 2009. *One Ring Circus: Dispatches from the World of Boxing* (Tucson, Arizona: Schaffner Press).

Hauser, Thomas. 2001. *A Beautiful Sickness: Reflections on the Sweet Science* (Fayetteville: University of Arkansas Press).

—. 1991. *Muhammad Ali: His Life and Times* (New York: Touchstone).

Holmes, Larry with Phil Berger. 1998. *Larry Holmes: Against the Odds* (New York: St. Martin's Press).

McCain, John with Mark Salter. 2002. *Worth the Fighting For: A Memoir* (New York: Random House).

Plimpton, George. 2003. *Shadow Box: An Amateur in the Ring* (Guilford, Connecticut: The Lyons Press).

Roosevelt, Theodore. 2004. *An Autobiography* (New York: Library of America).

Rotella, Carlo. 2003. *Cut Time: An Education at the Fight* (Boston: Houghton Mifflin Company).

Wiley, Ralph. 2000. *Serenity: A Boxing Memoir* (Lincoln and London: University of Nebraska Press).

Rollins on the Road

My review of the following tour diary for *The Brooklyn Rail* (February 2007) appeared under the title "Road Rollins":

Rollins, Henry. 2006. *A Dull Roar: What I Did on My Summer Deracination 2006* (Los Angeles: 2.13.61).

Going off Course with Melville & Liebling

Two writers I am extremely fond of share digressive tendencies. Liebling's invocation of Melville's most celebrated novel provided me with an excuse to pair the two authors in a consideration of their wide-ranging techniques. *Open Letters Monthly* published the essay in February 2009.

James, Clive. 2007. *Cultural Amnesia: Necessary Memories from History and the Arts* (New York: W.W. Norton & Company).

Liebling, A.J. 1990. *A Neutral Corner* (San Francisco: North Point Press).

—. 1956. *The Sweet Science* (San Francisco: North Point Press).

Melville, Herman. 1851. *Moby-Dick; Or, The Whale,* edited by Harrison Hayford and Hershel Parker (New York: W.W. Norton & Company, 1967).

—. 1849. *White Jacket; Or the World in a Man-of-War* (New York: Meridian, 1988).

Dedicated Writers

"Dedicated Writers," a slightly different version of which was published by the *Humanist* magazine (July/August 2008), refers to several works' dedication pages, which can be easily located in various editions. Below are the books and articles discussed in detail or quoted in the essay.

Brockman, John. 2006. *What We Believe but Cannot Prove: Today's Leading Thinkers in the Age of Certainty* (New York: Harper Perennial).

Docx, Edward. 2007. "To whom it may concern," *Telegraph,* 9 June, http://www.telegraph.co.uk/arts/main.jhtml? xml=/arts/2007/06/09/nosplit/bodocx109.xml.

Dowling, Tim. 2007. "This book is dedicated to ... who exactly?" *The Guardian,* 21 June, http://books. guardian.co.uk/news/articles/0,,2107907,00.html.

Hitchens, Christopher. 2007. *God Is Not Great: How Religion Poisons Everything* (New York: Twelve).

—. 2002. *Why Orwell Matters* (New York: Basic Books).

James, Clive. 2007. *Cultural Amnesia: Necessary Memories from History and the Arts* (New York: W.W. Norton & Company).

Lethem, Jonathan. 2007. "Edward's End," *New York Times Book Review,* 3 June, http://www.nytimes.com/ 2007/06/03/books/review/Lethem-t.html? _r=1&sq=lethem%20mcewan&st=nyt&oref= slogin&scp=1&pagewanted=print.

McEwan, Ian. 2007. *On Chesil Beach* (New York: Nan A. Talese).

—. 2005. *Saturday* (New York: Nan A. Talese).

—. 1997. *Enduring Love* (New York: Nan A. Talese).

—. 1987. *The Child in Time* (New York: Anchor Books).

Parker, Ian. 2006. "He knew he was right," *The New Yorker,* 16 October, http://www.newyorker.com/archive/2006/10/16/061016fa_fact_parker?printable=true.

Rushdie, Salman. 2002. *Step across This Line: Collected Nonfiction 1992 – 2002* (New York: Random House).

The Fighting Life
Boxing may not be the main event in the works discussed in this essay, but it does play a pivotal supporting role. Novelists like Philip Roth and Norman Mailer craft plots and develop characters through deft use of boxing history and insight into the qualities boxers often possess. *Philip Roth Studies* published the essay with the title "The Fighting Life: Boxing and Identity in Novels by Roth and Mailer."

Ellison, Ralph. 1952. *Invisible Man* (New York: Vintage Books).

Homer. 1974. *The Iliad,* translated by Robert Fitzgerald (Garden City, NY: Anchor Books).

Leeds, Barry H. 2008. "He Was a Fighter: Boxing in Norman Mailer's Life and Work." *The Mailer Review,* Vol. 2, No. 1, fall. 385-395.

Mailer, Norman. 2008. *Miami and the Siege of Chicago: An Informal History of the Republican and Democratic Conventions of 1968* (New York: New York Review Books).

—. 2003. *The Spooky Art: Some Thoughts on Writing* (New York: Random House).

—. 1984. *Tough Guys Don't Dance* (New York: Ballantine Books).

—. 1975. *The Fight* (New York: Vintage International).

—. 1965. *An American Dream* (New York: Dial).

—. 1959. "The Time of Her Time." *Advertisements for Myself* (New York: Putnam).

Margolick, David. 2005. *Beyond Glory: Joe Louis vs. Max Schmeling, and a world on the Brink* (New York: Alfred A. Knopf).

Mead, Chris. 1986. *Champion: Joe Louis: Black Hero in White America* (London: Robson Books).

McRae, Christopher. 2002. *Heroes without a Country: America's Betrayal of Joe Louis and Jesse Owens* (New York: Ecco).

Jones, Thom. 1993. *The Pugilist at Rest* (Boston: Back Bay Books).

Oates, Joyce Carol. 2002. *On Boxing*, expanded edition (New York: Ecco).

Plimpton, George. 2003. *Shadow Box: An Amateur in the Ring* (Guilford, Connecticut: The Lyons Press).

Roth, Philip. 2009. *The Humbling* (Boston: Houghton Mifflin Harcourt).

—. 2007. *Exit Ghost* (Boston: Houghton Mifflin Company).

—. 2000. *The Human Stain* (London: Vintage).

Rotella, Carlo. 2003. *Cut Time: An Education at the Fight* (Boston: Houghton Mifflin Company).

Schaap, Jeremy. 2005. *Cinderella Man: James J. Braddock, Max Baer, and the Greatest Upset in Boxing History* (Boston: Houghton Mifflin Company).

Torres, José, and Bert Randolph Sugar. 1971. *Sting Like a Bee: The Muhammad Ali Story* (Chicago: Contemporary Books).

Virgil. 1985. *The Aeneid,* translated by Allen Mandelbaum (New York: Bantam Books).

Ward, Geoffrey C. 2004. *Unforgivable Blackness: The Rise and Fall of Jack Johnson* (New York: Alfred A. Knopf).

Is Martin Amis Serious?

This essay reviews both Martin Amis's *The Second Plane* and many of the generally hostile reviews of it. (*Open Letters Monthly* published it in July 2008.)

Amis, Martin. 2008. *The Second Plane: September 11: Terror and Boredom* (New York: Alfred A. Knopf).

Donadio, Rachel. 2008. "Amis and Islam," *The New York Times Book Review,* 9 March, http://www.nytimes.com/2008/03/09/books/review/Donadio-t.html?sq=martin amis&st=nyt.

Fischer, Tibor. 2003. "Someone needs to have a word with Amis," *Telegraph,* 4 August, http://www.telegraph.co.uk/opinion/main.jhtml?xml=%2Fopinion%2F2003%2F08%2F04%2Fdo0404.xml.

Kakutani, Michicko. 2008. "Novelist's crash course on terror," *The New York Times,* 8 April. http://www.nytimes.com/2008/04/08/books/08kaku.html?scp=4&sq=the+second+plane&st=nyt.

—.2003. "Women may be from Venus, but men are from hunger," *The New York Times,* 28 October. http://query.nytimes.com/gst/fullpage.html?res=9F0CE1D71131F93BA15753C1A9659C8B63&scp=5&sq=martin+amis+yellow+dog&st=nyt.

Kirsch, Adam. 2008. "The writing man's burden," *The New York Sun,* 26 March, http://www.nysun.com/arts/writing-mans-burden.

Mason, Wyatt. 2008. "Afraid to go to the toilet," *Harper's Magazine/Sentences*, 14 May, http://www.harpers.org/archive/2008/05/hbc-90002934.

Orwell, George. 2002. *Essays,* edited by John Carey (New York: Everyman's Library).

—. 1946. "Why I Write" in Orwell, 2002, *Essays.*

—. 1945. "Politics and the English Language" in Orwell, 2002, *Essays.*

Perloff, Marjorie. 2008. "Martin Amis and the boredom of terror," *Times Literary Supplement,* 13 February. http://entertainment.timesonline.co.uk/tol/arts_and_entertainment/the_tls/article3363824.ece.

Sleeper, Jim. 2008. "A literary prophet's bad faith," *Talking Points Memo,* 27 April, http://tpmcafe.talkingpointsmemo.com/2008/04/27/it_takes_one_to_know_one/.

—. 2008. "'The Second Plane' by Martin Amis," *Los Angeles Times,* 14 April, http://www.latimes.com/features/books/la-et-book14apr14,0,7149217.story.

Tomasky, Michael. 2008. "Second thoughts: Martin Amis looks at the post-9/11 world," *Bookforum,* April/May, http://www.bookforum.com/inprint/015_01/229.

Taylor, Christopher. 2008. "Beware the nut-rissole artists," *The Guardian,* 26 January, http://books.guardian.co.uk/print/0,,332241803-110738,00.html.

Wieseltier, Leon. 2008. "The catastrophist," *The New York Times Book Review,* 27 April, http://www.nytimes.com/2008/04/27/books/review/Wieseltier-t.html?_r=1&sq+martin amis&st=nyt.

Write, Repeat
Combative polemicist Christopher Hitchens's frequent self-quotation in his journalism has parallels in diverse works of

fiction, poetry and scholarship by various writers. "Write, Repeat" (published by *Open Letters Monthly* in October 2008) examines how writerly recycling operates as creative repetition in works by Hitchens as well as boxing writer A.J. Liebling, novelist E.L. Doctorow and others.

Doctorow, E.L. 1994. *Waterworks* (New York: Random House).

—. 1984. *Lives of the Poets* (New York: Random House).

Greenblatt, Stephen. 2007. "Writing as performance," *Harvard Magazine,* September – October, pp. 40-47.

Hitchens, Christopher. 2008. "A man of incessant labor," *The Weekly Standard*, 10 March, Vol. 13, Issue 25, http:// www.weeklystandard.com/Content/Public/Articles/ 000/000/014/820eibyp.asp.

—. 2007. "The Grub Street years," *The Guardian*, 16 June, http://books.guardian.co.uk/print/ 0,,330033098-110738,00.html.

— (ed.). 2007. *The Portable Atheist: Essential Readings for the Nonbeliever* (Philadelphia: Da Capo Press).

—. 2007. *God Is Not Great: How Religion Poisons Everything* (New York: Twelve).

—. 2006. *Thomas Paine's* Rights of Man: *A Biography* (New York: Atlantic Monthly Press).

—. 2004. *Love, Poverty, and War: Journeys and Essays* (New York: Nation Books).

—. 2003. "The Permanent Adolescent," The Atlantic Monthly, May, http://www.theatlantic.com/doc/200305/ hitchens.

—. 2002. "Minority Report: Taking Sides," *The Nation*, 14 October, http://www.thenation.com/doc/20021014/ hitchens.

—. 2002. *Why Orwell Matters* (New York: Basic Books).

—. 2001. "Minority Report: Images in a Rearview Mirror," *The Nation*, 3 December, http://www.thenation.com/doc/20011203/hitchens

—. 2001. *Letters to a Young Contrarian* (New York: Basic Books).

—. 2000. *Unacknowledged Legislation: Writers in the Public Sphere* (London: Verso).

—. 1995. *The Missionary Position: Mother Teresa in Theory and Practice* (London: Verso).

—. 1993. *For the Sake of Argument* (London: Verso).

Liebling, A.J. 1990. *A Neutral Corner* (San Francisco: North Point Press).

—. 1956. *The Sweet Science* (San Francisco: North Point Press).

McEwan, Ian. 1987. *The Child in Time* (New York: Anchor Books).

McSmith, Andy. 2008. "From left to right: on the mid-life political conversions," *Independent,* 15 March, http://www.independent.co.uk/news/uk/politics/from-left-to-right-on-the-midlife-political-conversions-796267.html.

Messud, Claire. 2006. *The Emperor's Children* (New York: Alfred A. Knopf).

Oppen, George. 2003. *Selected Poems,* edited by Robert Creeley (New York: New Directions).

Said, Edward W. 2000. *Reflections on Exile: And Other Essays* (Cambridge: Harvard University Press).

Waugh, Alexander. 2004. *Fathers and Sons: The Autobiography of a Family* (New York: Nan A. Talese).

George & Me

Not every one of the works listed below is directly cited in "George & Me," which *Open Letters Monthly* published in May

2008, though most of them are. Every one of them contributed to my thinking about George Orwell, his work and his character after I read about the accusation of attempted rape made against him. The title, ampersand and all, deliberately mirrors that of Jacintha Buddicom's 1974 memoir. The postscript by Dione Venables added to the 2006 edition, and press reports related to it, prompted the research and reflection recorded in the essay.

Bowker, Gordon. 2007. "Blair Pounces," *Times Literary Supplement,* 23 February, http:// entertainment.timesonline.co.uk/tol/ arts_and_entertainment/the_tls/tls_selections/ commentary/article2305924.ece.

—. 2003. *George Orwell* (London: Abacus).

Buddicom, Jacintha. 1974. *Eric & Us,* with postscript by Dione Venables (Chichester: Finlay Publisher, 2006).

Hitchens, Christopher. 2002. *Why Orwell Matters* (New York: Basic Books).

Kermode, Frank. 2007 "The Sharpest Thorn," *The New York Review of Books,* June 14, pp. 46-48.

Meyers, Jeffrey. 2000. *Orwell: Wintry Conscience of a Generation* (New York and London: W.W. Norton & Company).

Orwell, George. 2002. *Essays,* edited by John Carey (New York: Everyman's Library).

—. 1949. *Nineteen Eighty-Four,* 1949 (London: Secker & Warburg).

—. 1945. "Freedom of the Press (*Animal Farm*)" in Orwell, 2002, *Essays.*

—. 1945. "Notes on Nationalism" in Orwell, 2002, *Essays.*

—. 1946. "Why I Write" in Orwell, 2002, *Essays.*

—. 1937. *The Road to Wigan Pier* (San Diego: Harcourt).

—. 1936. *Keep the Aspidistra Flying* (San Diego: Harcourt).

—. 1935. *A Clergyman's Daughter* (San Diego: Harcourt).

—. 1933. *Down and Out in Paris and London* (San Diego: Harcourt).

Spurling, Hilary. 2002. *The Girl from the Fiction Department: A Portrait of Sonia Orwell* (New York: Counterpoint).

Taylor, D.J. 2003. *Orwell: The Life* (New York: Henry Holt and Company).

Ink

Clive James boasts that *Cultural Amnesia* "might well be the only serious book to explore the relationship between Hitler's campaign on the eastern front and Richard Burton's pageboy hairstyle in *Where Eagles Dare*...." I could similarly suggest that "Ink," which debuted in print in *Spot Literary Magazine* (Vol. 2, No. 1, Spring 2008), probably stands alone among personal essays by combining contemplation of car crashes, jaguars, Camus, the Bad Brains, tattoos, boxing, T.E. Lawrence and Bond girls.

BOOKS AND ARTICLES DISCUSSED

Bauer, Edwin A. and Peggy Bauer. 2003. *The Last Big Cats: An Untamed Spirit* (Stillwater, Minnesota: Voyageur Press).

Blakeslee, Sandra. 2006. "Gone for decades, jaguars steal back to the Southwest," *The New York Times,* 10 October, http://www.nytimes.com/2006/10/10/science/10jaguar.html?sq=jaguar%20and%20arizona&st=nyt&scp=1&pagewanted=print.

Camus, Albert. 2006. *Camus at* Combat: *Writing 1944 – 1947,* edited by Jacqeuline Lévi-Valensi; translated by Arthur Goldhammer (Princeton: Princeton University Press).

—. 1947. *The Plague,* translated by Stuart Gilbert, in *The Plague, The Fall, Exile and the Kingdom, and Selected Essays* (New York: Everyman's Library).

D'Abo, Maryam and John Cork. 2003. *Bond Girls Are Forever: The Women of James Bond* (New York: Harry N. Abrams).

National Highway Traffic Safety Administration (NHTSA). 2006. *Traffic Safety Facts 2005* (Washington, DC: NHTSA).

Newfield, Jack. 2002. *Somebody's Gotta Tell It: The Upbeat Memoir of a Working-Class Journalist* (New York: St. Martin's Press).

Todd, Olivier. 1998. *Albert Camus: A Life,* translated by Benjamin Irvy (New York: Alfred A. Knopf).

FILMS DISCUSSED

Die Another Day, directed by Lee Tamahori (2002).

The Living Daylights, directed by John Glen (1987).

Octopussy, directed by John Glen (1983).

The Spy Who Loved Me, directed by Lewis Gilbert (1977).

Thunderball, directed by Terence Young (1965).

Goldfinger, directed by Guy Hamilton (1964).

Lawrence of Arabia, directed by David Lean (1962).

RECORDINGS DISCUSSED

Bad Brains. 1996. *Black Dots* (Caroline Records, CAR 7534).

—. 1983. *Rock for Light* (Caroline Record, CAROL1613-2).

—. 1982. *Bad Brains* (Reachout International Records, RUSCD8223).

Weight Loss: A Love Story

Despite a couple references to books by Kingsley and Martin Amis, the personal essay "Weight Loss: A Love Story" does not rely on others' texts. What I say about diabetes and how to cope with it does reflect my understanding of the *American Diabetes Association Complete Guide to Diabetes,* 4th edition. Ian MacKaye spoke at the Independent and Small Press Book Fair in New York City on December 1, 2007. A version of the essay first appeared in *Blood and Thunder* in fall 2009.

Fighters & Writers

"Fighters & Writers" surveys a small but representative selection of the mammoth body of boxing literature and literature involving boxing in addition to writing on closely related topics such as confidence games. The hybrid of a personal essay and a critical review first appeared in *The Mailer Review* (Vol. 2, No. 1, fall 2008). While it relies heavily on the books listed below, it began to germinate with a conversation with José Torres and Paul Johnson at the Tribeca Grill in January 2002 and subsequent discussions with them.

Camus, Albert. 1955. *The Myth of Sisyphus and Other Essays,* translated by Justin O'Brien (New York: Vintage Books).

Campbell, Jeremy. 2001. *The Liar's Tale: A History of Falsehood* (New York: W.W. Norton & Company).

Hauser, Thomas. 1991. *Muhammad Ali: His Life and Times* (New York: Touchstone).

Heinz, W.C. 1958. *The Professional* (Cambridge: Da Capo Press).

Kahn, Roger. 1999. *A Flame of Pure Fire: Jack Dempsey and The Roaring '20s* (San Diego: Harcourt).

Liebling, A.J. 1990. *A Neutral Corner* (San Francisco: North Point Press).

Mailer, Norman. 2003. *The Spooky Art: Some Thoughts on Writing* (New York: Random House).

—. 1975. *The Fight* (New York: Vintage International).

Maurer, David. W. 1940. *The Big Con: The Story of the Confidence Man* (New York: Anchor Books).

Musil, Robert. 1953. *The Man without Qualities, Volume I: A Sort of Introduction,* translated by Eithne Wilkens and Ernst Kaiser (New York: Perigee Books).

Newfield, Jack. 2002. *Somebody's Gotta Tell It: The Upbeat Memoir of a Working-Class Journalist* (New York: St. Martin's Press).

—. 1995. *Only in America: The Life and Crimes of Don King* (New York: William Morrow and Company).

Oates, Joyce Carol. 2002. *On Boxing*, expanded edition (New York: Ecco).

Rendell, Jonathan. 1997. *This Bloody Mary Is the Last Thing I Own: A Journey to the End of Boxing* (Hopewell, New Jersey: The Ecco Press).

Strauss, Darin. 2002. *The Real McCoy* (New York: Dutton).

Torres, José, and Bert Randolph Sugar. 1971. *Sting Like a Bee: The Muhammad Ali Story* (Chicago: Contemporary Books).

INDEX

Adams, Maud, 149
Ali, Muhammad, v-vii, xi-xii, 1-16,
    17, 19, 22-26, 48-49, 59,
    75-76, 87, 92, 97, 99, 102,
    114, 171-176, 178, 181,
    183
Allen, Woody, 13
Amis, Kingsley, 80, 82, 107, 112,
    157
Amis, Martin, xi-xii, 77, 80-82,
    105-115, 158, 166
Archilochus, 117, 129
Arkush, Michael, 2-4, 7-16
Ashe, Arthur, 4, 6
Association of Boxing
    Commissions, 38
Atlas, Teddy, 15, 47, 52
Austen, Jane, 61

Bad Brains, 152-153
Baer, Max, 27-31, 91, 93, 95
Barnes, Julian, 81
Bauer, Edwin, 148
Bauer, Peggy, 148
Bellow, Saul, 109, 114
Berbick, Trevor, 22, 25
Berger, John, 119-120
Berlin, Isaiah, 129
Berry, Halle, 149
Bin Laden, Osama, 110-111
Bingham, Howard, 76
Blair, Eric (see Orwell, George)
Blueford, Jerry, 48
Borges, Jorge Luis, 63
Bowker, George, 135-139
Braddock, James J., v-vi, 27-31, 93
Brunt, Stephen, 23
Buddicom, Guinever, 136-138, 140
Buddicom, Jacintha, 135-139
Bush, George H.W., 119
Bush, Geroge W., 113, 128
Byron, George Gordon, Lord, viii

Cain, Sim, 57

Caine, Michael, 13
Campbell, Frankie, 30
Campbell, Jeremy, 173
Camus, Albert, vii-viii, xii-xiv, 60,
    153-154, 169, 179-180
Canzoneri, Tony, 86
Carnera, Primo, 29-31
Carpentier, George, xiii
Césaire, Aimé, 126
Chavez, Jesus, 41-43
Chomsky, Noam, 122
Chuvalo, George, 26
Clay, Cassius (see Ali,
    Muhammad)
Connolly, Cyril, 22
Conquest, Robert, 82
Cooper, Henry, 25
Cosell, Howard, 8
Costello, Frank, 85-86, 103

D'Abo, Maryam, 149
Dahl, Roald, 119-120
D'Amato, Cus, 18-19, 21, 25, 47,
    172-173, 176, 183
De La Hoya, Oscar, 31
Dempsey, Jack, viii, 173
Dickens, Charles, 124
Doctorow, E.L., 125-126
Docx, Edward, 75-76
Donadio, Rachael, 112
Donne, John, 78
Dostoevsky, Fyodor, 122
Douglas, Alfred, x
Douglas, James "Buster," 20, 22,
    29
Dowling, Tim, 77
Dundee, Angelo, 7
Dunn, Katherine, 20, 52
Durham, Yank, 8

Eagleton, Terry, 112
Early, Gerald, 23
Egan, Pierce, ix, 126
Eliot, George, 122

Eliot, T.S., 9, 129
Ellis, Jimmy, vi
Ellison, Ralph, 96-97, 102

Farr, Tommy, 31
Fenton, James, 81
Fischer, Tibor, 106
Fleming, Ian, 149
Foreman, George, xi, 19, 23, 24,
    26, 59, 87, 174, 176,
    178-179
Franco, Francisco, 132-133
Frazier, Joe, xi, 2-3, 6, 8-9, 14, 15,
    24, 148, 152, 153, 173, 179
Fugazi, 168
Futch, Eddie, 173

Galento, Tony, 86
Gallico, Paul, viii
Gast, Leon, 23
Gatti, Arturo, 46
Gibbon, Edward, 126
Gibbs, Melvin, 57
Givens, Robin, 19
Goodman, Margaret, 42-44
Gould, Joe, 27
Greenblatt, Stephen, 124, 126
Guevara, Ernesto "Che," 11
Gumbel, Bryant, 4

Haley, Alex, 14-15
Haskett, Chris, 57
Hauser, Thomas, 4, 8-12, 14-15,
    50-51, 75-76, 173-174
Hawthorne, Nathaniel, ix, 62-64,
    67-70, 82
Haygood, Wil, 143
Heeney, Tom, viii
Hegel, Georg Wilhelm Friedrich,
    127
Heinz, W.C., 55, 181-182
Hemingway, Ernest, viii, 84, 180
Hitchens, Christopher, ix, 77-82,
    117-124, 126-129, 135
Hitler, Adolf, 91, 93-94, 133

Hoffman, Philip Seymour, 114
Holmes, Larry, 24, 49, 51, 53
Holyfield, Evander, 20-21
Homansky, Flip, 42-44
Homer, 83, 97-98, 102
Horace, 76

International Labor Office, 35,
    38-39

Jack, Beau, 95
Jackson, John, viii
James, Clive, 63-65, 80, 82, 158,
    166
Jefferson, Thomas, 127
Jennings, Shooter, 131
Jewish War Veterans, 93
Johansson, Ingemar, 71-73
Johnson, Jack, vi
Johnson, Leavander, 41-44
Johnson, Paul, 172, 180
Jones, Thom, 99

Kahn, Roger, 173
Kakutani, Michiko, 105-106, 109,
    111-113, 115
Kant, Immanuel, 66
Kelly, Gene, 13
Kelly, Ray, 46-47
Kempton, Murray, 171
Kennedy, Edward, 13
Kermode, Frank, 134-136, 139-140
Khomeini, Ayatollah Ruhollah,
    118
King, Don, 19-20, 178
King, Martin Luther, Jr., 7-8, 10-11
Kirsch, Adam, 107, 109, 112
Kissinger, Henry, 127
Kitchen, Neil, 78
Kram, Mark, 8, 11-12, 14
Ku Klux Klan, 5, 16
Kundera, Milan, 102

Lahiri, Jhumpa, 75
Larkin, Philip, 82

Lawrence, T.E., 153-154
Le Carré, John, 119-120
Ledger, Heath, 114
LeDuff, Charlie, iii-iv
Leeds, Barry H., 87, 100
Lethem, Jonathan, 78
Lewis, Lennox, 20
Liebling, A.J., viii-ix, xiii-xiv, 8-9,
    22-23, 61, 70-73, 125, 126,
    173, 180
Limbaugh, Rush, 14
Liston, Sonny, 5, 7, 22, 25
Locke, John, 66
Long, Earl, xiii
Louis, Joe, v, vi, xiii, 2, 6, 31,
    92-95, 172
Lyle, Ron, 24-25

Mack, Luther, 44
MacKaye, Ian, 161, 168
Mailer, Norman, iii-iv, viii, ix-xii,
    xiv, 1-2, 8-9, 13, 83-89, 91,
    92, 99-100, 102, 114, 171,
    176-180
Mallory, Thomas, 126
Malloy, Dallas, 52
Mamet, David, 175
Manso, Peter, iv
Marciano, Rocky, viii, 71-73, 86,
    92
Margolick, David, 91, 93
Marino, George, 42-44
Marquis of Queensbury, x-xi, 17,
    22
Marqusee, Mike, 4-5, 10-12, 14
Marshall, Joshua Micah, 109
Martin, Joe, 49
Marx, Karl, 67, 117, 124, 127, 128
Mason, Wyatt, 109
Mauer, David, 174-175
McCain, John, 46, 48, 51
McCormack, Peter, 19
McCoy, Charles "Kid" (see Selby,
    Norman)
McEwan, Ian, 77-81, 122, 126-127

McIlvanney, Hugh, vi, vii
McLemee, Scott, 106
McRae, Donald, 93-94
Mead, Chris, vi, 92-94
Melville, Herman, viii-ix, 61-73,
    82, 175
Mencken, H.L., 122
Messud, Claire, 125
Meyers, Jeffrey, xii, 135
Minor Threat, 161
Moore, Archie, viii, 71-73, 100-101
Moorer, Michael, 47
Morris, Lewis, xv
Muhammad, Elijah, 5-7, 12
Munford, Harvey J., 44
Musil, Robert, 173

Namath, Joe, 13
Nation of Islam, 5-7, 9-11, 16, 22
National Collegiate Athletic
    Association, 51
National Highway Traffic Safety
    Administration, 147
Nave, James, 44
Nevada State Athletic
    Commission, 38, 42, 44
Newfield, Jack, 148, 152, 178-180
Non-Sectarian Anti-Nazi League,
    93
Norton, Ken, 24

Oates, Joyce Carol, iv, x, xiii, xiv,
    4, 85, 180
O'Brien, "Philadelphia" Jack, viii
Olmsted, Frederick Law, 158
Oppen, George, 125
Orwell, George, xii, 79, 82, 101,
    109-111, 113, 120, 124,
    129, 131-142
O'Toole, Peter, 153

Pacheco, Ferdie, 7
Paine, Thomas, 127
Parker, Dan, 28
Parker, Ian, 80

Patterson, Floyd, 18, 71-72, 172
Pep, Willie, 172
Perloff, Marjorie, 106, 111, 115
Plimpton, George, viii, xiii, 49-50,
      52, 83, 84, 100-101, 103,
      172

Qaeda, al-, 133

Rahman, Jimmi, 75
Reed, Ishmael, 172
Remnick, David, 5, 10-11, 16
Rendell, Jonathan, 175-176,
      180-181
Rizzo, Frank, 3
Robinson, Sugar Ray, 143, 172
Rogich, Sig, 44
Rollins, Henry, vii, 57-60
Roosevelt, Theodore, 45-49, 51-52
Ross, Diana, 13
Rotella, Carlo, vi, viii-ix, x, xiv, 50,
      97-98
Roth, Philip, ix-x, 83-84, 88-92, 95,
      97-103
Ruggeroli, Charles, 44
Ruiz, John, 31
Rushdie, Salman, 77, 80-81,
      118-120, 123, 127

Said, Edward, 126
Salinger, J.D., 75, 80
Sammons, Jeffrey T., x
Schaaf, Ernie, 30
Schaap, Jeremy, 28-31, 93
Schiller, Friedrich, 122
Schmeling, Max, v-vi, 2, 92-95
Schulberg, Budd, viii, 1, 13, 33
Selby, Norman, 182
Shakespeare, William, 78, 111, 122
Shavers, Earnie, 24
Shawn, William, 75
Silverglade, Bruce, 51-52, 184
Sinatra, Frank, 11, 13, 106
Sleeper, Jim, 106, 111, 113-114
Smith, Red, 29-30

Smith, Zadie, 75
Sontag, Susan, 119
Soyinka, Wole, 172
Spinks, Leon, 24
Spinoza, Benedict de, 66
Steward, Emanuel, 48
Stillman, Lou, 101
Strauss, Darin, 182-183
Sugar, Bert Randolph, 1, 86, 172
Swift, Jonathan, 76

Talese, Gay, 172
Taliban, 133
Taylor, Christopher, 106, 109, 111,
      113
Taylor, D.J., 131, 135
Teresa, Mother, 121
Terhune, Albert Payson, viii
Thompson, Hunter S., 172
Toback, James, 17-18, 21, 26
Tolstoy, Leo, 122
Tomasky, Michael, 106, 109,
      111-113
Torres, José, iii-iv, ix, xii, xiv, 1-2,
      4, 6-7, 9, 19, 21, 86, 102,
      171-173, 175-176, 178,
      183
Trevor-Roper, Hugh, 119-120
Tunney, Gene, viii
Twain, Mark, 76, 124
Tyson, Mike, v, x, 17-22, 23, 24,
      25-26, 29, 47, 172, 175

United Nations, 35, 149
United Service Organization, 58

Van Rock, Theo, 57
Vaux, Calvert, 158
Venables, Dione, 135-140, 142
Virgil, 76, 83, 98, 171, 183

Ward, Geoffrey C., vi, ix, 96
Ward, Mickey, 46
Washington, Desiree, 19
Waugh, Alexander, 128

Waugh, Evelyn, 128-129
Wieseltier, Leon, 105, 109-110,
    113-114
Wilde, Oscar, x, 21
Wiley, Ralph, 48, 51
Wodehouse, P.G., 124, 126, 128
Wolfe, Tom, 172

X, 57, 60
X, Malcolm, 5, 7, 8, 11, 25

Zola, Émile, 124

John G. Rodwan, Jr.'s writing has been published by *The American Interest, The Mailer Review, Blood and Thunder, Fight News, Spot Literary Magazine, Open Letters Monthly, The Oregonian, Free Inquiry, The Humanist* and *The Brooklyn Rail,* among others. Raised in Detroit, Michigan, he earned a master's degree in English from Wayne State University. He has lived in Geneva, Switzerland, and Brooklyn, New York, and currently resides in Portland, Oregon.

Breinigsville, PA USA
11 October 2010
247139BV00005B/1/P